P9-CNC-368

=HOW TO=
INVEST
$50-$5,000

Third Edition

NANCY DUNNAN

Harper Perennial
A Division of HarperCollins Publishers

This book is sold with the understanding that neither the Author nor the Publisher is engaged in rendering legal or financial services. Questions relevant to the practice of law or personal finance should be addressed to a member of those professions.

The Author and Publisher specifically disclaim any liability, loss, or risk, personal or otherwise, which is incurred as a consequence, directly or indirectly, of the use and application of any of the contents of this work.

HOW TO INVEST $50–$5,000 *(Third Edition)*. Copyright © 1991 by Cloverdale Press, Inc. All rights reserved. Printed in the United States of America. No part of this book may be used or reproduced in any manner whatsoever without written permission except in the case of brief quotations embodied in critical articles and reviews. For information, address HarperCollins*Publishers*, 10 East 53rd Street, New York, New York 10022.

FIRST HARPERPERENNIAL EDITION

Library of Congress Cataloging-in-Publication Data

Dunnan, Nancy.
    How to invest $50–$5,000 / Nancy Dunnan.—3rd ed., 1st HarperPerennial ed.
    p. cm.
    ISBN 0-06-273004-5
    1. Investments—Handbooks, manuals, etc. I. Title. II. Title:
How to invest fifty to five thousand dollars. III. Title: How to
invest fifty dollars to five thousand dollars.
HG4527.D77   1991
332.6′78—dc20   90-55497

91 92 93 94 95 CC/MB 10 9 8 7 6 5 4 3 2 1

CONTENTS

INTRODUCTION:

Getting the Most for Your Money

A fool and his money is soon parted.
—English proverb

This book is intended to help you keep your money, whether you have only a few dollars or a few thousand. Most people, regardless of their income, don't know how to save or, if they do save, what to do with their money/savings. Consequently, they and their money part ways.

Perhaps you're a new or small investor, or you have money sitting in an account somewhere earning just 5¼ percent. . . . Maybe you're just starting out on your first job. . . . Maybe you've saved several hundred dollars from your summer work . . . or several thousand dollars from careful budgeting. . . . You received a sudden windfall so that for the first time in your life you have a lump sum to invest. . . . You got a bonus . . . or you have a business that's taking off. . . .

Even if you have only a small amount to invest, you should start now—today; for the sooner you begin, the sooner your $50, $500, or $5,000 will grow. Think about it: If you invested $500 at the end of each year at 8 percent compounded annually, at the end of five years you would have $2,933. At the end of ten years you would have $7,243. You too can watch your money grow through wise investment.

Sometimes small investors feel their options are limited. They're not. More than two dozen investment vehicles are described in detail in this book. We will show you how to take advantage of each one.

In fact, you'll soon discover that all the financial world is wooing you and your money. Banks, brokerage firms, insurance companies, and financial planners are vying for your cash—be it $50 or $5,000. In fact, every major financial institution has a new gimmick to entice the novice as well as to hold on to the seasoned client.

We'll explain which ones are best, which ones are safest, which ones will give you the best return. You will learn that a savings account at your corner bank is no longer the only option for the small investor. In this handbook, we will teach you to feel comfortable moving your money around, from one investment to another as your needs change, as interest rates and the economy change. The right place for your first $50 won't be the right one for your first $500 or $5,000.

Although those of us with up to $5,000 constitute the nation's largest group of investors it's not easy to find information explaining how to tailor personal needs to specific investment instruments. Most money books address people in high-income brackets—those who can afford a financial planner to guide their every move.

This book will change all that for you. It will fill that void by covering the specific concerns of those who have a maximum of $5,000 to invest. It will tackle the fact that in today's climate no one type of investment works well all the time; that reading the changes in interest rates is crucial; that diversification will minimize financial pitfalls; and, finally, that liquidity and the ability to move assets quickly are essential in a changing economic climate.

How to Invest $50–$5,000 will carefully guide you through the maze of money vehicles, teaching you how to develop the art of smart decision making. You will learn to tackle Wall Street and your bank with confidence and self-assurance. We won't tell you which stock to buy, which bond is best, or even which bank to use, but we will show you how to analyze your options as you watch your money grow from $50 to $5,000. Cutting through the jargon and getting right down to the basic facts, *How to Invest $50–$5,000* will explain things financial so that no matter how inexperienced you are, you soon will feel comfortable deciding where to put your investment dollars.

Being a good investor, however, takes time and knowledge. But if you follow our step-by-step plan, you'll soon know exactly what to do and when. Make a point of setting aside some time to learn about handling your money, to explore the world of finance. It's worth the time and effort for one simple reason: No one cares as much about your money as you do!

Begin by reading the box that follows called "The Ten Dumbest Mistakes People Make About Money." You'll soon see you're not alone in shying away from investing, in putting off saving. Second, put a check next to those mistakes that are yours. Third, reread the suggested solutions for each mistake. They are simple and easy to follow. Fourth and finally, resolve to take action today—or at least before the end of the month!

THE TEN DUMBEST MISTAKES PEOPLE MAKE ABOUT MONEY

---

1. *Being ashamed to invest small amounts.* With this attitude, you'll never save anything. What is small to one investor may be huge to another. *Solution:* Begin saving something from the next income or salary check you receive. The dollar amount is not important. Developing the habit of saving is. Read "Nine Easy/Painless Ways To Save" in the Appendix.

2. *Having inadequate emergency savings. Solution:* Stash six months' worth of take-home pay in a money market mutual fund or interest-bearing checking account. Read Chapters 6 and 7.

3. *Leaving cash in a regular bank savings account. Solution:* Move it immediately to a money market fund or a money market deposit account. Read Chapters 7 and 14.

4. *Operating too many accounts.* If you have several bank, mutual fund, and brokerage accounts you're spending too much on service fees. And it's hard to keep track of interest rates and other details. *Solution:* Consolidate. Have one checking account, one or two money market funds and brokerage accounts.

5. *Not knowing whether an investment is for current income or for appreciation.* In general, a growth stock or growth mutual fund should not be expected to pay high current income while a CD, bond, or utility stock should not be purchased in anticipation of price appreciation. *Solution:* Read Chapters 11 and 15.

6. *Avoiding financial goals.* Yogi Berra said it best: "If you don't know where you're going, you're probably going to wind up

(con't)

someplace else." Most people spend more time planning their vacations than their financial future. Consequently, they spend as much or more on cruises, airline tickets, and hotels than they do funding their retirement accounts or building up a nest egg. *Solution:* Determine one or two specific financial goals. Write them down or discuss them with a stockbroker or financial advisor. Preferably, do both.

7. *Failing to diversify.* People often put all their money in one place because it's convenient, it's familiar, or they're just plain lazy. No investment is sufficiently profitable or safe to justify this approach. *Solution:* Divide your assets among banks, mutual funds, stocks, bonds, etc.

8. *Procrastinating.* People put off making financial decisions because they're afraid they'll do the wrong thing. *Solution:* Set time deadlines and take several small, conservative investment steps, one at a time. For example, if you have $2,000, in week number one, put half the money into a money market account. The next week, buy a CD. The following week, put the rest into a blue chip stock.

9. *Ignoring savings plans at work.* Tax-deferred plans, such as 401(k) or stock purchase plans, are usually good deals, especially if the company matches your contribution. *Solution:* Talk to your benefits officer *this week.* Read Chapters 12 and 13.

10. *Failing to have a will.* Estate planning is critical if you care about other people. *Solution:* Write your will this weekend.

PART ONE

Safe Stashing for Your First $50

1
Institutional Cookie Jars: Banks

In your great-grandmother's day, the family savings were tucked away in a cookie jar, stuffed under the mattress, or hidden in a deep hole behind the back porch. People of your grandmother's generation, who lost money when many of the banks closed their doors in 1929, may still be putting their faith and their money in the land, just as Scarlett O'Hara's daddy advised.

Yet for most of us, a savings account at the local bank still seems the most logical holding spot for that first $50. But not necessarily. Let's take a look at what your bank will do with your $50 and what other options you have.

Selecting a Bank

Not all banks are created equal, nor do all banks treat all customers equally. So, don't make a mad dash to the first bank on your corner. It pays to shop around, even with just $50 burning a hole in your pocket. Eventually you will become a larger depositor and will need to use the bank for other reasons—a loan, a mortgage, or a checking account. Some banks offer estate planning, courses in financial planning, and computerized investing—all services you may want later on.

Since most Americans are always in a hurry, the single most common factor in deciding where to bank is, of course, location. Yet, your nearest branch is not necessarily the right choice for you. Before opening a savings account, check out your neighborhood bank, by all means, but also make personal visits to several others. Don't worry about the quality of the wall-to-wall carpeting or the abundance of fresh flowers. Decor is, of course, not the issue. But other things certainly are.

Check to see:

- If all types of services are offered
- How well rush hour traffic is handled
- If there are express lines
- If there are branches near both where you live and where you work
- If there are bank officers accessible to answer questions, or if you are likely to be sent scurrying from one desk to another in a Kafkalike circle
- If there is written material available on interest rates and service charges

The last point is especially important when selecting a **commercial bank,** a **savings and loan association (S&L),** or a **credit union** for your savings. Before we go any further, let's establish the differences among the three.

S&Ls were originally called building and loan associations. Members pooled their savings so that they could borrow money to build houses. Today, S&Ls continue to specialize in home mortgages and often pay slightly higher interest on savings than commercial banks.

Commercial banks offer the widest range of services of all depository institutions. Initially they serviced only businesses, but starting in the early part of this century they began to solicit accounts from people from all walks of life. Today they offer every conceivable type of account, loan, and service.

Credit unions emerged in this country in the early 1900s to help those working class people who didn't qualify for loans from commercial banks. The members of a credit union pooled their money and made low-interest loans to one another. Today credit unions serve those with a common bond (see pages 10–11 for more on these institutions).

Although banks are free to pay whatever rate they choose, most offer 5¼ or 5½ percent on savings accounts. Credit unions sometimes pay as much as two percentage points higher.

The stated rate, however, is only the tip of the iceberg. It is also important to know exactly how often the interest will be paid, because every time your account is credited with interest, you will have that much more money to calculate on the next time interest is paid. In other words, the more frequently interest is *compounded*, the more money you will earn.

So, open your account at a bank where interest is compounded daily; it will provide a better return than if interest is compounded quarterly. In turn, quarterly is better than semiannually.

Despite the many and confusing ways in which bankers manage to figure interest on their savings accounts, your $50 is better off there than in the cookie jar because the temptation to put your hand in and spend it is greatly reduced—and, you will actually earn a modest rate of interest.

Passbook and Savings Accounts

Banks offer two types of savings accounts: **passbook accounts** and monthly **statement accounts.** In order to open either type, call or visit your bank and ask about its minimum deposit requirement. In a small-town bank it may be only $5, while a larger bank may require $100 or more. With a passbook account, savers receive a thin booklet in which the bank records all deposits, withdrawals, and interest payments after each transaction. Many banks have done away with the passbook, however, and instead record all transactions only in the bank's computer. This account, the statement savings account, provides savers with a printed monthly statement detailing all transactions. Its advantage: You do not have to worry about losing your passbook.

Most banks have either a passbook or a statement type account and do not give you a choice. Some, however, have both, paying a slightly higher interest rate on statement accounts because they are less expensive for them to operate.

Fees

In many banks, if your balance falls below a certain amount, you will be assessed a monthly charge or you will lose interest, or possibly both. For example, a bank may require a $500 minimum to open a statement savings account, on which it will pay 5½ percent, but if your balance falls below $500, a monthly fee of $1.50 is slapped on. So you could actually lose money because of the monthly charge! Or the bank may have a passbook savings account, available for as little as $5, but it pays only 4½ percent. Check these details carefully when selecting a bank for your first $50. And remember, if your account is inactive, meaning you have not made a deposit or withdrawal during a certain time period, banks typically charge a small monthly fee.

Yield

Banks often advertise two figures: the annual interest rate and the effective yield. The difference between the two comes from how often interest is credited to your balance, thus increasing the principal on which interest is paid. A 5 percent interest rate has an effective annual yield of 5 percent if the interest is credited annually. If it is credited quarterly, the effective yield is 5.094 percent, and if interest is credited monthly, 5.116 percent.

BANK SAVINGS ACCOUNT

For Whom

- Small saver
- Those with less than $500

Where to Open

- Bank
- Savings and loan association

Fees and Minimum Balance

- No opening fee
- Monthly fees vary if balance drops below certain level

Safety Factor

- High
- Deposits insured up to $100,000 at all FDIC (Federal Deposit Insurance Corporation)-insured institutions.

Advantages

- Safety
- Geographically accessible
- Withdrawal upon demand
- Principal is guaranteed up to $100,000 by federally backed insurance corporation if bank is FDIC insured.

Disadvantages

- Interest rate is low and fixed.
- Checks cannot be written.
- Monthly fees on low balances may mean you will lose money.

Coupon Clubs

It's certainly gimmicky, but if it helps you save, then give the bank coupon club a try.

The coupon club is the generic name for a myriad of programs devised by banks to attract business. These include Christmas clubs, Hanukkah clubs, vacation clubs, and so forth. Also offered by savings and loan associations and credit unions, they are especially popular with those who like tearing coupons out of books.

If you decide to join one, each week or month, depending upon the club, you will make a specified deposit or payment, enclosing a coupon with your money. At the end of a stated period, usually a year, your coupons will all be gone and your account full of money. In some clubs you cannot withdraw your money until the stated period is over.

Couponless Plans

In some banks, you can sign up for automatic savings deposit plans if you make the arrangements. You designate the monthly amount you want to save, let's say $35. This amount is then automatically taken out of your checking account and deposited into your savings account. Interest rates, which are fixed, vary—4 to 5½ percent is standard. The record of your transaction is then attached to your regular checking account statement.

COUPON CLUBS

For Whom

- Undisciplined savers
- People with large families who have to buy lots of holiday gifts
- Those who like tearing along perforated lines

Fee

- Usually none

Safety

- High

Advantages

- Forced way to save

Disadvantages

- Some clubs pay low interest or no interest at all.
- Some pay interest only if you complete the full term of the club.
- You may not be able to withdraw your money until the full year is over.

ATMs

Automated teller machines, electronic machines located in bank lobbies, shopping centers, and on street corners across America, provide instant access to money 24 hours a day. To use an ATM you need an encoded plastic card, which is inserted into the machine, and a personal identification number, issued by the bank.

Although ATMs are a godsend on weekends and when bank lines are long, use them with discretion:

- Check to see whether your bank charges for each ATM transaction.
- Very often cards issued by one bank may be used in the ATM of another bank, but for a fee.
- Use a bank that is part of an ATM network, such as MAC, MOST, NYCE, SAM, STAR, or CIRRUS, in which case you can use your ATM when you're out of state or even overseas.
- Visa and MasterCard can be used in many ATMs for cash advances. *Caution:* You pay interest on these advances from the minute you receive the cash.
- Time your withdrawals. If you want money from your bank's money market deposit account where it's earning interest, make your withdrawal by ATM after 3 P.M., the bank's official closing hour. That way you'll get the maximum interest.

Hint: Each bank sets a limit on how much cash you can withdraw on any one day. If you're planning to get cash for a trip, check the daily limit first.

Ways to Get the Most Out of Your Bank

New electronic systems, revised banking rules, and expanded marketing programs all mean better deals for savvy bank customers. Read the examples below and then talk to your banker. These and other "deals" are not always advertised.

- Currency exchange. Get an exchange rate bargain by using a bank's automated teller machine (ATM) card to purchase foreign currency. Your Plus or CIRRUS card, issued by U.S. banks that are members of one of those ATM networks, may be used at nearly 10,000 banks around the world to withdraw local currency. The machine dispenses currency at an exchange rate that is 3 to 5 percent less than the official retail rate. And you don't pay the 2 to 5 percent added transaction cost that many banks charge for accepting U.S. dollar traveler's checks.

- Buyer protection plan. Goods purchased by Visa or MasterCard are protected by a 90-day replacement insurance.
- Senior citizens' programs. Free checking, no-fee credit cards, free traveler's checks, and discounts on tickets to cultural events for "older" customers.
- Warranty bonus. Doubles the warranty for up to one year on any purchase paid for by check, and gives 90-day protection against loss, breakage, theft, or fire for these purchases. Claims usually cannot exceed $50,000 per year. People with homeowner's insurance can collect only what their insurance does not cover. Some items are generally excluded: cars and artwork, for instance. To make a claim, you call a toll-free number for a form, which you submit with a copy of your check, sales receipt, and, if the product carries one, warranty.
- Fees waived. Customers who combine deposits and loans and keep a minimum balance don't pay service charges.

A Bank Checkup

- Ask your banker how interest is compounded.
- Get a printed chart of interest rates to study at home.
- Ask if the bank pays interest only on the lowest balance during the quarter. For example, if you have $200 in your account and you take out $75, then eventually build it back up to $200, is interest paid as though you had only $125 in the account all the time?
- Look for a bank paying interest from day of deposit to day of withdrawal.
- Will you be charged extra if you make many withdrawals?
- Are there any days at the end of the quarter when interest is not paid?
- How many days are in the bank's year? (Some banks have "dead days" at the end of a quarter when they don't pay interest.)
- If you take out money, or close the account at mid-quarter, will you lose interest?

- Are there penalties for leaving your account inactive for a long period?
- Is there a monthly service charge?

Study carefully the chart on annually compounded interest in a $50 account and use it as a guideline for making your banking decision.

$50 COMPOUNDED AT 5 1/2 PERCENT

	In 1 Year	In 5 Years	In 10 Years	In 20 Years
Daily	$ 53.73	$ 71.66	$ 102.71	$ 211.00
Monthly	52.82	65.85	86.73	150.43
Quarterly	52.81	65.77	86.51	149.68
Semiannually	52.79	65.58	86.02	147.99
Annually	52.75	65.35	85.41	145.89

How Safe Is Your Bank?

The recent rash of bank failures has made even the most financially reckless aware of the importance of safety. There's no need to tuck your money under the mattress, but you should:

1. Bank only at federally insured institutions. Look for the FDIC sign at the bank. It stands for Federal Deposit Insurance Corporation, an independent agency of the U.S. Government that was established by Congress in 1933 to insure bank deposits. Member banks pay for the cost of insurance through semiannual assessments based on the volume of deposits.

2. Keep in mind that individual depositors, not accounts, are insured—up to $100,000, including interest and principal. That means if you have two accounts in the same name in one bank, you are insured only for $100,000, not $200,000.

3. Find out how safe your bank really is. For a modest fee, Veribanc, Inc., will send you a financial evaluation of any bank or savings and loan. Contact Veribanc, Inc., at P.O. Box 461, Wakefield, MA 01880; 617-245-8370.

4. For information on FDIC insurance, call the consumer hotline at 800-424-5488, or write the Office of Consumer Affairs for a free copy of "Your Insured Deposit" at 550 117th Street NW, Washington, DC 20429.

2
Credit Unions

Once thought of only as a place for assembly line workers to get a car loan, **credit unions** have taken on a brand new look. They are a viable choice for your $50, and they usually pay one to two percentage points above bank rates. There is no lid on interest rates; they vary from union to union.

Credit unions are cooperatives, or not-for-profit associations of people who pool their savings and then lend money to one another. By law, they must have so-called "common bonds," which may consist in working for the same employer, belonging to the same church, club, or government agency, or even living in the same neighborhood. Because they are not-for-profit and because overhead costs are low, credit unions almost always give savers and borrowers better rates and terms than commercial institutions.

There are more than 15,000 U.S. credit unions with assets in excess of $200.5 billion. While the largest, the Navy Federal Credit Union, has 1.04 million members, the average has 2,000.

Today's upbeat union bears very little resemblance to the cooperatives established some seventy-five years ago in order to save working-class people from the ubiquitous loan shark. These feisty cooperatives have aggressively expanded their turf, offering a line of sophisticated financial services and often competing very favorably with commercial banks and savings and loans. Many, in fact, operate like local banks.

Theoretically, unions are run by the depositors—every member, in fact, must be a depositor, albeit a very small one, although the true organizational work is done by volunteer committees in the smaller unions and by paid employees in the larger groups.

If you are not already a member of a credit union, but would like to be one, write to the industry's trade organization for a list of the unions you might be able to join:

Credit Union National Association
P.O. Box 431
Madison, WI 53701

But before you invest your $50 in a credit union:

- Make sure the union is insured by the National Credit Union Share Insurance Fund, a federal agency.
- Inquire about its reputation from members.

If you are interested in starting a credit union, contact the CUNA, or check the telephone book for the nearest regional office of the National Credit Union Administration. This group supervises and insures federal credit unions. Or write to the National Association of Federal Credit Unions, P.O. Box 3769, Washington, DC 20007, for a free copy of "Share a Common Interest: Sponsor a Union."

CREDIT UNIONS

For Whom

- Members and members' families

Where to Find

- Your place of work
- Your neighborhood association
- Church, club, synagogue

Minimum

- You must buy at least one share to join a credit union.
- Shares are determined by each union and vary from $5 to $30, with most around $15. (A share is really your first deposit.)

Safety

- Varies, but generally above average

Advantages

- Interest rates on savings are generally higher than at commercial institutions.
- Interest rates on loans are generally lower than at commercial institutions.
- Other services may be offered, such as mortgages, credit cards, checking accounts, IRAs, CDs.
- An automatic payroll deduction savings plan is frequently available.
- Purchase of stocks listed on the New York Stock Exchange and other exchanges is possible at low commissions.

Disadvantages

- Might be run by inexperienced volunteers or inadequately staffed
- Might not be adequately insured
- May not return canceled checks

3
Uncle Sam &
Savings Bonds

The bank isn't the only safe slow-growth investment vehicle for your $50. Uncle Sam is willing and eager to keep it for you and, in return, provide a little something in the way of interest through what is known as a **U.S. Savings Bond.** When you buy a U.S. Savings Bond you are lending money to the U.S. Government.

A few years ago, the government savings bond program was known as the dog of the investment world. It played upon the heartstrings of all good Americans, using the theme of patriotism to lure in the money. Often, low-income families sank all they had into savings bonds only to end up earning interest well below average. When inflation, for instance, was at 10 percent, the government was paying a measly 6.5 percent—hardly something the Treasury officials could have been proud of.

Since then, the program has been revamped, revised, and remarketed. Now the Series EE Savings Bonds are a viable way to save small amounts of money (known as preserving capital) and at the same time earn interest.

You can buy EE bonds at your bank in multiples of $25. The purchase price is actually 50 percent of the bond's face value, so in other words, a $50 bond costs only $25. (EE Savings Bonds are sold in the following face value amounts: $50, $75, $100, $200, $500, $1,000, $5,000, and $10,000.) If you hold them until maturity, you'll get back the face value, $50 per bond in the case of a $25 bond, plus variable interest. In addition to buying these bonds at the bank, you may also buy them through automatic payroll deductions, as thousands of employers participate in the savings bond program. This is a good way to save if you're not a natural saver. In fact, after a while you may not even miss the $25 from your paycheck.

These bonds pay 4.16 percent for the first six months and 4.27 percent for the first year. Then, the yield rises every six months up to five years. After that, you earn interest equal to 85 percent of the average yield on five-year Treasury notes. The government guarantees a minimum of 6 percent on all EEs held for five years. (On November 1, 1986, the minimum guaranteed rate was cut from 7.5 to 6 percent. EE bonds bought before that date continue to earn the old rate of 7.5 percent over the bond's life.)

If you redeem your bond between six months and five years after purchase, you will get back your full investment, that is face value of bond, plus the earned interest.

If you cash in your bond before five years are up you won't earn the top rate of interest. Here's the current schedule:

- Between 1 and 1½ years, the rate is 4.43 percent
- Between 1½ years and 2 years, the rate is 4.64 percent
- Between 2 and 2½ years, the rate is 4.82 percent
- Between 2½ and 3 years, the rate is 5.01 percent

- Between 3 and 3½ years, the rate is 5.26 percent
- Between 3½ and 4 years, the rate is 5.5 percent
- Between 4 and 4½ years, the rate is 5.76 percent
- Between 4½ and 5 years, the rate is 6 percent

You cannot, however, redeem your bond *at all* during the first six months. For the current rate on bonds held five years or more, telephone 800-US-BONDS. This rate changes each November 1 and May 1.

EE SAVINGS BONDS

For Whom

- Those who won't need the money until five years have passed
- Those who want a competitive deferred yield
- Those who have a low tolerance for risk and want to be certain that their principal is safe

Where to Purchase

- Banks
- Payroll savings plan
- Savings and loan associations
- Credit unions
- Federal Reserve Bank (see addresses on page 65)
- Bureau of the Public Debt, Securities Transaction Branch, Washington, DC 20226

Fee and Minimum

- No fee
- Minimum purchase, $25 for a $50 bond

Safety Rating

- Highest possible

Advantages

- Virtually no risk because the principal is government-backed and interest is default proof

- Easy to buy at your local bank

- No commission or sales fee

- Income is exempt from state and local taxes.

- Federal tax can be deferred until bonds are redeemed or mature.

- EE bonds are an excellent way to save for a child's education, especially if you can target them to come due after he or she reaches age 14, at which point the interest income will be taxed at the child's lower rate. Until the child turns 14, however, earned investment income from assets given to the child by a parent are taxed at the parent's presumably higher rate.

- EE bonds purchased after January 1, 1990, by a bondholder at least age 24 and used to pay college tuition are free from federal income tax provided you fall within certain income guidelines when the bonds are redeemed. Ask your local bank for details.

- Upon maturity, you may reinvest, or roll over, your Series EE Savings Bonds into Series HH bonds and further defer your taxes until the HH bonds mature, another ten years down the road. HH bonds can be purchased only by rolling over EE bonds that have reached maturity and are available in denominations of $500.

PAYING FOR COLLEGE

The earlier you start saving, the more you will have when your child is ready for college. This information, from the Bureau of Public Debt, assumes an annual interest rate of 6 percent; the actual rate may be higher or lower, which would affect the total saved.

Child's Age When Savings Start	Monthly Investments of $50	$100
	Will Grow to These Amounts by Age 18:	
1 year old	$ 17,356.08	$ 34,712.16
6 years old	10,328.96	20,657.92
10 years old	6,025.72	12,051.44
12 years old	4,226.88	8,453.76

4
Mini-Investor Programs

Once you have tucked away a small nest egg, then $50, believe it or not, can move you into the stock market. There are several interesting programs especially designed for the mini-investor; but remember, stocks are more risky than any of the previously mentioned vehicles. These mini-programs are not designed to take the place of a savings account. They are merely an inexpensive way to buy stocks. Participation is suggested only after you have saved at least three months' living expenses for an emergency.

Unfortunately, many brokers who once welcomed small investors discourage them today by charging high commissions on small trades. For example, 100 shares of a $50 stock will cost between $97 and $108 in brokerage commissions from "full-service" firms like Merrill Lynch, Shearson Lehman Hutton, Paine Webber, and so forth. A discount firm, on the other hand, charges around $49 for the same purchase. (Full details about buying stocks can be found in Chapter 17.)

Yet, there are several ways you can get into the action with your $50 and at a reasonable rate.

Buying Stock Directly

You can bypass stockbrokers altogether by going directly to the company to buy stock. Only a handful of public companies offer this unique service, but you can expect more to join the bandwagon. Contact the Shareholder Relations Division at:

W. R. Grace & Company
1114 Avenue of the Americas
New York, NY 10036
212-819-5500

Johnson Controls, Inc.
5757 North Green Bay Avenue
Milwaukee, WI 53202
414-228-1200

The Kroger Company
1014 Vine Street
Cincinnati, OH 45202
513-762-4000

American Recreation Centers, Inc.
9261 Folsom Boulevard
Sacramento, CA 95826
916-362-2695

At press time, American Recreation Centers stock was available only to residents of California and Texas.

Barnett Banks of Florida
Customer Stock Purchase Plan
P.O. Box 2507
Jacksonville, FL 32231

You must have an account at a Barnett Bank to buy shares directly.

You can purchase stock directly from these companies, if you live in an area serviced by the following utility companies:

Carolina Power & Light   Idaho Power
Central Hudson Gas & Electric   Montana Power
Central Maine Power   Portland General Electric
Cleveland Electric Illuminating   Puget Sound Power & Light
Dominion Resources   San Diego Gas & Electric
Duke Power   Union Electric

Hint: If there is a company you're interested in, you can inquire by writing to it directly. Address your letter to the Shareholder Relations Department.

Dividend Reinvestment Plans

It Pays To Be a DRIP

No one likes to pay brokerage commissions, even to a friendly broker. In fact, they prevent some small investors from buying stocks at all. There's one way around this dilemma: Over a thousand companies permit existing shareholders to participate in a DRIP (Dividend Reinvestment Program). These plans allow investors who already own stock in a company to buy additional shares by automatically reinvesting their dividends. Many are solid blue chip companies (such as AT&T, Clorox, Du Pont, Heinz, and Kellogg) or public utilities that pay above-average dividends. Although some companies do charge a nominal fee, most don't charge a typically heftier brokerage commission. Many also offer 3 to 5 percent off the market price of new shares, so you're really paying a lower price than you would through a stockbroker. Many also allow shareholders to make cash payments into the plan to accumulate more shares in their accounts.

Hint: If you already own stock in a company, call the Shareholder Relations Division and ask if the company has a DRIP. Before asking for a prospectus and application, however, find out how many shares you need to enroll. With some companies, a single share is sufficient; others require 15, 50, or 100 shares.

For a complete listing of companies with DRIPS, contact Dow Theory Forecasts, Inc., 7412 Calumet Ave., Hammond, IN 43624-2692; 219-931-6480; cost: $4.95.

SELECTED STOCKS WITH REINVESTMENT PLANS

Plans With No Discount

Consolidated Edison	Travelers
General Motors	Ford
U.S. West	NYNEX
Atlanta Gas & Light	Wisconsin Energy
Eastman Kodak	BellSouth
Exxon	IBM
Kimberly-Clark	American Home Products

Plans With a 5 Percent Discount

Citizens & Southern	Signet Banking
Southeast Banking	Fleet/Norstar
Security Pacific	MNC Financial

Plans With a 3 Percent Discount

Bank of Boston	Citicorp
J.P. Morgan	

Two More Low-Cost Ways To Buy Stocks

- *Buying One Share.* Individual investors may join the National Association of Investment Clubs. (NAIC's address and more information are found on page 23). Under NAIC's "Low-Cost Investment Plan" for a one-time charge of $5 per company, you can buy as little as one share directly from more than 60 major participating corporations, including Disney, Kellogg, McDonald's, Mobil, and Quaker Oats. Most do not charge a commission, although a few require a nominal fee ($2 to $3) for each transaction to cover expenses. Most have Dividend Reinvestment Programs.

- *Buying at Work.* An increasing number of companies offer plans through which employees can buy stock in the company called ESOPs, or Employee Stock Ownership Plans. Check with your personnel division to see if your employer offers this option. According to the Employees Benefit Research Institute, the most popular plan is one that permits employees to contribute up to 6 percent of their salary and then the firm matches half that contribution.

The Blueprint Program

An inexpensive and convenient way for you to invest in stocks has been devised by Merrill Lynch, the nation's largest full-service brokerage firm. Through the Blueprint Program, you can now invest any dollar amount you want, the initial minimum being $100. The interesting aspect of this program is that you're investing by the dollar amount, not by the share, which means you can acquire fractions of shares as well as whole units. You may buy any stock that trades on the New York and American Stock Exchanges and many over-the-counter stocks. Merrill Lynch's list of recommended stocks for participants in the Blueprint Program, updated periodically, will be sent to participants upon request. It consists of stocks with above-average dividend yields or long-term growth potential.

Blueprint Program participants get a break on commissions. The firm charges up to 55 percent less than regular Merrill Lynch fees on stock transactions.

BLUEPRINT PROGRAM

For Whom

- Any small investor interested in getting into the market with minimal expenditures

Where to Purchase

- Your local Merrill Lynch office, or from:

    The Blueprint Program
    Box 30441
    New Brunswick, NJ 08989-0441
    800-637-3766

Minimum and Fees

- $100

- Commission is discounted by 55 percent from regular fees.

Safety Factor

- Like any stock purchase, safety depends on the price changes in the stock.

Advantages

- Low entry cost

- Merrill Lynch research and professional assistance

- Diversification

- Liquidity

- Reduced brokerage fees

- Optional automatic dividend reinvestment plan

- Company annual report will be sent to you as soon as you have one full share of any security.

- Record keeping and tax data are taken care of by Merrill Lynch.

- Dollar cost averaging

Disadvantages

- Risk is equal to that of the stock market.

DOLLAR COST AVERAGING

While no investment plan is risk-free, dollar cost averaging, a technique offered by the Blueprint Program, can help cushion you from stock market fluctuations. With dollar cost averaging you invest the same fixed dollar amount every month in the same stock. That means you buy more shares when prices go down and fewer when prices go up. Over the long run, you get a lower average cost per unit for the investments you make. *Note:* You can cancel this plan at any time. You can also use dollar cost averaging on your own or with mutual funds.

5

Investment Clubs

Of all the options you have at your doorstep, a clubhouse will provide you with the most fun and enjoyment—if not the greatest return on your principal—as a home for your $50.

Joining an investment club is an excellent way to learn about the stock market, the movement of interest rates, and the overall economy. It is also a great way to meet new people who, like you, are interested in learning how to handle a small amount of money.

Most clubs are small—optimum size is about twenty—and they meet once or twice a month in a community center or in a member's home. Members pool their money and jointly purchase shares of stock. Clubs require monthly payments that can range from $20 per month to as high as the members dare go. Energetic hosts frequently combine the regular business meeting and discussion with coffee, dessert, or other refreshments.

The mechanics are simple. Making money, though, is not—especially if most members are inexperienced. Nevertheless, you will get your investment feet wet, and by combining your collective dollars and knowledge, who knows—you might pick a winner or two!

If you don't know of a club in your area, ask at work or at a local YMCA or YWCA, adult education center, church, or synagogue. If you cannot find a club to join, start your own with a few friends or colleagues. The steps are easy:

1. Find twelve to twenty people willing to join a club. Set the minimum investment requirement ahead of time—$25 per month is common.

2. Select a person to be responsible for paper work. This task should rotate every few months.

3. Contact the National Association of Investment Clubs, 1515 East Eleven Mile Road, Royal Oak, MI 48067, 313-543-0612, for details on how to get started. Your club may join this association for $30, plus $9 per member. You will receive a stack of useful literature plus a subscription to *Better Investing* magazine. The NAIC also gives advice on organizing, conducting meetings, analyzing stocks, and setting up portfolios. Individuals can join NAIC for $32.

4. Establish firm guidelines regarding withdrawal of a member's funds and entry of new members.

5. Meet and invest on a regular basis—whether or not the market is doing well.

6. Reinvest all earnings in a diversified portfolio—one that has at least five different companies.

7. Use a discount broker to save on commission fees.

8. Stick to regular stock buy-and-sell procedures. All members should be responsible, on a regular, rotating basis, for doing research and making recommendations to the club.

INVESTMENT CLUBS

For Whom

- Anyone

Minimum

- Set by individual clubs. Ranges from $20 per month up. Members contribute the set amount on a monthly basis.

Safety Factor

- Depends on the club's philosophy

Advantages

- Inexpensive and supportive way to learn about investing

- Reduces anxiety surrounding first-time investing and selling

- Individual members of the NAIC can buy one share of any of a number of companies and thereafter invest small amounts periodically (see pages 19–20).

Disadvantages

- You may earn a better return elsewhere, especially if your club is inexperienced.

- Results are not guaranteed.

- Investment is not insured.

- High mortality rate—many clubs fail in the first twelve to eighteen months.

HOW YOUR $50 WILL GROW

	One Year	Five Years	Ten Years
Commercial Savings Bank (5¼% compounded daily)	$ 52.63	$ 54.86	$ 71.67
S & L Association (5.5% compounded daily)	53.73	71.66	102.71
EE Savings Bond (6% compounded semiannually)	52.16	67.20	90.32
Coupon Club (6% compounded monthly)	53.08	67.44	90.97

PART TWO

The First $500

6

Interest-Paying Checking Accounts

Until recently, the advantage of having cash—that is, money in your pocket or in your savings account—was that it provided a reserve and was there, available immediately, whenever you needed it. But you probably never harbored any wild notions that you would make a lot of money with your idle cash, just a little interest from the bank. But in the last decade or so intense competition for savers' money has forced banks to pay interest on checking accounts.

Therefore, holding cash itself has turned into an investment choice and has taken on new meaning within the financial world. There are now a number of investment choices for holding cash:

- Interest-paying checking accounts
- Treasury bills, notes, and bonds
- Money market mutual funds
- Insured bank money market deposit accounts
- Bank certificates of deposit (CDs)

26

checking

First, let's take a look at interest-paying checking accounts, sometimes called **NOW accounts.** NOW stands for Negotiable Order of Withdrawal. These are like regular checking accounts with printed checks and regular statements, but they *also* pay interest—5¼ percent generally. They are simply a handy housekeeping account that permits you to earn a little interest on your cash balance as you pay bills. Sounds good. But there are several caveats attached. In order to earn the 5¼ percent, a minimum or monthly average balance must be maintained. These minimums vary nationwide from about $300 to several thousand dollars.

If you fall below the required minimum balance, you will lose interest and you may also be subject to per-check, per-deposit, and/or monthly charges.

The equivalent of this account at a credit union is called a **share draft.** Since credit unions do not have a cap on the amount of interest they can pay, share drafts generally offer slightly higher rates than bank accounts.

Before opening an interest-paying checking account, quiz your banker and get precise answers to these questions:

- How is the minimum balance determined? Most banks add up your balance at the end of each day. If you're short, even for one day, you're slapped with a full service fee.

- If you fall below the minimum, what will you be charged? Banks have devised several clever ways of addressing this question. Some charge you for every check written during the month; others only for those written during the time when you were below minimum requirements. Another variation on the theme: You'll be charged only if you write more than a certain number of checks, say fifteen or twenty. Regardless of the methods used by the bank, it pays to have this type of account only *if* you keep up the balance.

- How is the interest figured? Again, as in a passbook savings account (see pages 3–5), you will get the best deal if your interest is figured from day of deposit to day of withdrawal, or on your daily average balance.

In the competitive banking world of today, an interest-paying checking account is a good choice *if* you can maintain the minimum amount in order to avoid having to pay steep fees and charges that eat up any earned interest. But do your calculations carefully. If you know maintaining the balance will be difficult, you will be better off with a regular checking account.

INTEREST-PAYING CHECKING ACCOUNTS

For Whom

- Ideal for anyone who wants a checking account and can maintain the bank's minimum balance at all times

Minimum

- Varies from around $300 to $3,000 or more

Safety Factor

- Insured up to $100,000

Advantages

- You can earn interest on a checking account.

- You can write checks of any amount.

Disadvantages

- Bank charges on regular checking accounts are almost universally lower than on these special accounts.

- Minimums for maintaining accounts are steep.

- Regular checking accounts sometimes toss in a few free extras, such as no charge for checks, toasters, and so forth. These don't.

After you have taken care of opening your checking account, the next $500 you accumulate should be transferred to one of the higher-paying parking places where you can earn almost twice as much interest as in a passbook savings account.

First we will examine the pros and cons of money market mutual funds and then we will move on to CDs, Treasury notes and bonds, and other high-yielding places for your money.

7
Money Market Mutual Funds

After you've opened a checking account, then saved $500, the next step is to find a safe place to put your hard-earned savings. One choice is a **money market mutual fund** where you can earn almost twice as much as in a regular savings or checking account. A money market mutual fund is really just a special kind of mutual fund—which, in turn, is an investment company. When you participate in a mutual fund you are buying shares in an investment corporation. This means that your investment dollars are pooled with those of hundreds of other investors and the combined total is invested by a professional manager in various investment vehicles. The fund manager studies the market, interest rates, and other economic indicators, buying and selling those investments that best suit the fund's stated aims or goals.

There's Power in Numbers

The value of a fund is that one large pool of money can be far more effectively invested than hundreds or thousands of small sums. Each investor, no matter how large or small his or her investment, then owns a proportional share of the fund, and receives a proportional return, without discrimination based on the number of shares owned.

There are many types of funds. Some are set up for long-term growth, some for immediate income, others for tax-free returns. Some are willing to take higher levels of risk than others. Some are devoted exclusively to buying and selling stocks; others to bonds, or a combination of the two.

In the case of a money market mutual fund, the goal is a high yield with minimum risk. Money market funds derive their name from the type of securites they invest in—"money market" securities.

Financial companies, large corporations, and the U.S. Government

29

all borrow large sums of money for short periods (one year or less) by issuing **money market securities** in exchange for cash. For example, the government borrows by way of Treasury bills (T-bills) and notes; large corporations by IOUs called commercial paper; and banks by way of large certificates of deposit called CDs.

These money market securities make up the fund's portfolio, rather than stocks and bonds.

The borrowers—the government, large corporations, and banks—are good risks. They consist of the country's most solid institutions, and they all agree to pay back the money quickly and at high rates. That's why today you can earn almost double the traditional passbook savings account rate.

Obviously no ordinary saver would be able to participate in this venture on his or her own. The amounts involved are too large. But through a money market mutual fund, many average investors can share in this opportunity at relatively minimal cost.

So, by pooling your money with other investors and purchasing these T-bills, CDs, and other money market securities, you can lend to large institutions and gain high yields because the money earned by the fund, after expenses, is in turn paid out to you, the shareholder, as interest or "dividends."

Although most funds require a minimum deposit of $1,000 some have lower opening amounts. Additional deposits are usually at least $100.

A key point in favor of these funds is their liquidity. You have almost immediate access to your money without penalty. You can cash in your shares by phone, by mail, or through your broker. And, most funds will wire money from the fund directly to your local bank.

In most funds, you can also tap the money by writing checks against your shares. Generally a fund permits unlimited check writing as long as the checks are for amounts over $500.

One fund that has an opening minimum of only $500 and will let you write checks for as little as $250 is:

Money Market Management
Federated Investors
Federated Tower
Pittsburgh, PA 15222-3779
800-245-2423—outside Pennsylvania
412-288-1948—in Pennsylvania

There are more than 300 of these money market mutual funds open to individual savers. For a complete list of money market and other funds, send $5.00 to:

> The Investment Company Institute
> 1600 M Street NW
> Washington, DC 20036
> 202-293-7700

This pamphlet contains the names, addresses, and toll-free telephone numbers as well as the initial and subsequent investment minimums of each fund.

If you have less than $500 to invest, you can still participate in a money fund. One fund has no minimum:

> Twentieth Century Cash Reserves
> P.O. Box 419200
> Kansas City, MO 64141
> 800-345-2021

Another fund has only a $250 minimum:

> Colonial Money Market Fund
> P.O. Box 1722
> Boston, MA 02015-1722
> 800-225-2365

Several funds have only $500 minimums for opening:

> Templeton Money Fund
> 800-237-0738

> Daily Cash Accumulation
> 800-525-9310

> Franklin Group Money Funds
> 800-342-5236

> Liberty Government Money Market Trust
> 800-245-4770

Call or write away for a copy of each fund's prospectus. This will tell you what investments are in the fund's portfolio as well as give an indication of its past performance. Money market funds and their yields are also listed in the newspaper.

In selecting a fund, ask yourself these questions:

- What minimum investment can I afford?
- Do I want a fund nearby, through my broker, or can I invest by telephone or by wire?
- How easily can I redeem my shares? What is the fund's policy about writing checks? Will the fund wire money to my bank? How long will it take?
- Can I transfer from this fund to another if the economic climate changes (see pages 90–93)?
- What types of securities does the fund invest in? Would I feel safe in a different type of fund, say one that invests only in government securities?

Pete has Fidelity Magellen

THE HIGHEST YIELDING MONEY MARKET FUNDS

Fund	Telephone	Minimum
Fidelity Spartan	800-544-6666	$20,000
Dreyfus Worldwide Dollar Money Fund	800-645-6561	2,500
Alger Portfolio	800-992-3863	1,000
Evergreen Trust	800-235-0064	2,000
Flex Fund	800-325-FLEX	2,500

WHAT KINDS OF THINGS MONEY MARKET FUNDS BUY

Agency securities. Issued by government agencies such as Government National Mortgage Association (Ginnie Mae) and the Small Business Administration or by government-sponsored organizations such as the Federal National Mortgage Association (Fannie Mae) and the Federal Home Loan Banks.

Bankers' acceptance. Commercial notes guaranteed by a bank.

Certificates of deposit. Large-denomination, negotiable CDs sold by both U.S. and foreign commercial banks and by some S&Ls.

Commercial paper. IOUs sold by corporations for day-to-day operating funds.

Eurodollar CDs. Dollar-denominated certificates sold by foreign branches of U.S. banks or by foreign banks.

Treasury bills and notes. Sold on a periodic basis by the U.S. Treasury and backed by the "full faith and credit" of the government.

Repurchase agreements. "Repros," buy-sell deals in which the fund buys securities with an agreement that the seller will actually repurchase them with in a short time—generally seven days or less—at a price that includes interest for that time. The fund holds the securities as collateral.

Yankee CDs. Certificates issued by U.S. branches of foreign banks.

Safety

How safe are money market funds? Although they are not federally insured, since they began in 1972 only one money market fund has ever failed: First Multifund of New York, which was paying an extremely high rate—93 cents on the dollar—back in 1979.

Two services provide continually updated professional rankings and safety ratings of the money market mutual funds. Call or write for complimentary copies of the following newsletters:

> "Income & Safety"   (monthly; $49/year)
> Institute for Econometric Research
> 3471 North Federal Highway
> Fort Lauderdale, FL 33306
> 305-563-9000; 800-327-6720

> "Donoghue's Moneyletter"   (twice monthly; $99/year;
> P.O. Box 6640   includes annual directory
> Holliston, MA 01746   of all money funds)
> 508-429-5930

If you are <u>concerned with safety</u>, you should select a fund that has a high portion of <u>U.S. Government securities</u> in its portfolio, as well as CDs from well-known domestic banks and top-rated commercial paper (e.g., IBM, General Electric, Exxon). You can find out about what is offered by writing or calling the fund and asking for a copy of the prospectus, which lists its investments.

The safest funds of all, of course, are those that invest *only* in U.S. guaranteed securities. You will certainly sacrifice a point or two in exchange for safety. Among the better known funds that invest exclusively in U.S. guaranteed securities are:

> Capital Preservation Fund
> Benham Group
> 1665 Charleston Road
> Mountain View, CA 94303
> 800-4-SAFETY

> Merrill Lynch Government Fund
> P.O. Box 9011
> Princeton, NJ 08543
> 800-282-2800

> Fidelity U.S. Government Reserves
> Fidelity Investments
> 82 Devonshire Street
> Boston, MA 02109
> 800-544-6666

> T. Rowe Price U.S. Treasury Money Market Fund
> T. Rowe Price
> 100 East Pratt Street
> Baltimore, MD 21202
> 800-638-5660

> Vanguard Money Market Trust Federal Portfolio
> The Vanguard Group
> P.O. Box 2600
> Valley Forge, PA 19482
> 800-662-7447

Hint: Don't pick a fund just because it has the word "government" in its name. That doesn't guarantee safety! Rather, it means that the odds are that the fund invests primarily in government securities. Unfortunately, however, not all funds are scrupulous about the meaning their name implies.

Another method for ensuring low risk is to select a fund with holdings of less than fifty days. In other words, if a fund's capital is invested in longer-term holdings and then if interest rates rise significantly, that fund's yield to you will be lower than that of funds holding shorter-term issues. In that event, a large number of fund owners might want to sell their shares in order to move into a higher-paying fund. In an extreme case—and it would indeed be extreme—the fund might be forced to sell assets at a loss.

Actually, money market mutual funds *are* quite safe. *They invest only in very short-term securities,* which helps them to maintain their liquidity and to insulate themselves from negative interest-rate movement. These securities usually mature in less than two months. And, by law, only 5 percent of a fund's assets may be held in obligations of any one institution other than obligations of the U.S. Government. This ruling further adds to the safety of the funds.

Tax-Exempt Money Funds

The dividends you earn on most funds are fully taxable. Some funds, however, invest solely in tax-exempt securities. Therefore their dividends are not taxed by the IRS, only by the state and local government.

A note of caution: Unless you are in a high tax bracket, it doesn't pay to buy into a tax-exempt fund (see chart, page 56). These funds have lower yields and generally pay about half the rate of regular funds.

For the day when your taxable income puts you in the 28 percent tax bracket, you may want to investigate:

Dreyfus Tax-Exempt Money Market Fund
800-645-6561

Franklin Tax-Exempt Money Market Fund
800-342-5236

Lexington Tax-Free Money Fund
800-526-0052

Triple Tax-Exempt Money Funds

If you live in a state with high income tax rates, you can get an even greater tax break from a fund in which interest earned is "triple tax-exempt," that is, free of local, state, and federal income taxes. A list regularly appears in the *Wall Street Journal* and *Money* magazine. Among the best known are:

> Fidelity *Massachusetts* Tax-Free Money Market
> 800-544-6666
>
> Pru-Bache *New York* Municipal Money Market Fund
> 800-222-4321
>
> Vanguard *California* Tax-Free Money Market Fund
> 800-662-7447
>
> Calvert Tax-Free *California* Portfolio
> 800-3368-2748
>
> CIGNA Tax-Exempt of *Connecticut*
> 800-572-4462
>
> Fidelity *Michigan* Tax-Free Money Market
> 800-544-6666

SHOULD YOU BUY A TAX-EXEMPT FUND?

To determine if a tax-exempt fund is worthwhile:

1. Subtract your tax bracket from the number 1.
   1 minus .28 = .72 ·

2. Then, divide the tax-free yield the fund is paying by .72 to find the taxable equivalent.

3. The result is the yield you'd need on a taxable investment to match the tax-free yield. For example, if a tax-free investment is yielding 5.5 percent, divide 5.5 by .72. The answer, 7.64, is the yield you'd need to beat with a taxable investment.

8
Certificates of Deposit

Certificates of deposit, called **CDs,** are time certificates sold by banks. They are issued for a specified amount of money for a specified period. If you are looking for safety and high yields, this is the place for you. You agree to leave a certain amount of money with the bank, S&L, or credit union for a stated amount of time, ranging from a few months to several years. When that time period is up, the CD "matures" or "comes due" and you get the full amount plus interest back.

Minimum deposits vary from several hundred dollars on up to several thousand dollars. Large CDs—those of $100,000 and up—are called **jumbo CDs.**

The Financial Services Revolution

CDs are a byproduct of the "revolution in financial services," which started in 1972 when the first money market mutual fund, The Reserve Fund, offered its shares to the public. Thus, the small investor got a taste of high interest rates for the first time. And for a minimum of only $1,000!

Until then, the only choices available to the investor with several hundred (or several thousand) dollars were a savings account and/or U.S. Savings Bonds—both paying measly returns.

For years, government rules made it virtually impossible for small savers to do much: Savings accounts had interest ceilings on them, and the higher-yielding commercial banks' CDs could be issued only in denominations of $100,000 or higher. Government restrictions prevented small depositors from pulling their money out of passbook savings accounts and putting it in CDs, because the feeling was that the banks might have trouble paying their many customers high CD market rates, since most of their assets at that time were in low-yielding mortgages. In the process of protecting the banks, the government penalized the small saver.

As the money market funds began to make significant inroads, however, taking small savers away from the banks, these venerable institutions demanded that the government lift their interest rate ceilings, all of which led to today's far more competitive, and deregulated, banking environment.

Differences Among Bank CDs

Because all banks are now free to bid for your money, it is crucial that you investigate as many as possible when looking for a CD. Don't assume they all have more or less the same rates, because it's just not true. Minimums vary. Rates vary. Compounding interest varies. Maturities vary.

In general, you will find that:

- Interest rates on similar CDs offered by different banks in the same city can vary by as much as one full percentage point.
- You will earn more on your CD if the interest is compounded daily.
- Some banks "tier" their interest rates, which means they pay higher interest on larger deposits.
- Banks can set any maturities they wish.
- Many banks will let you set your own maturity for what they call a "designer CD." If you have to prepare for college tuition, for instance, you can buy a CD that comes due when your child goes off to school in September.

When shopping for a CD, ask your banker about the institution's policy regarding penalties for cashing in a certificate before it matures. CDs of one year or less may carry a penalty of thirty-one days' interest. On deposits of one year or more, ninety days' interest is not unusual. Not all banks have the same penalties.

Depending upon where you live, and the number of area banks competing for your money, you will find that CD minimums range from about $500 to $1,000. For those that will mature in less than a year, $1,000 to $2,500 is standard. CDs that remain on deposit for over a year are often available for only $500. Watch for periodic local interest-rate wars and take advantage of temporarily higher rates.

CDs VERSUS OTHER CASH ALTERNATIVES

Vs. Money Markets
Although CDs of one year or less tend to pay slightly higher rates than bank money market accounts, you give up immediate access to your money.

Vs. Treasury Notes
Before you buy a longer-term CD, compare the rate to a Treasury note. An advantage of T-notes is that their interest is free from state and local taxes.

Buying a CD from Your Broker

As part of the trend toward one-stop financial shopping, you can buy a CD through a stockbroker. With a broker, you will get high yields as well as FDIC insurance, and you escape those hefty early-withdrawal penalties the banks impose.

When you buy a bank CD you agree to leave your money on deposit for a stated period—a few months to several years. If you want to get your money out, you have to pay a penalty. However, if you are attracted by high interest and low minimum investment and yet want to avoid the early-withdrawal penalties, a brokered CD is usually the right move.

Here's how it works. *First,* you tell your broker what CD maturity you want. He will quote a rate. Since the bank pays the broker to sell the CD, you will not be stuck paying your broker a commission. Then you proceed to buy the CD.

Second, if you want to redeem it before maturity, you can sell it back to the broker without a penalty—he can readily sell it to someone else in the "secondary market." However, the price of the CD will fluctuate depending upon what it's worth on the open market.

In general, your CD will go up in price if money market interest rates go down. It will decrease in value if money market interest rates rise. That means it is sometimes possible to make a profit by actually cashing in a CD early.

CHECKLIST

- Call two or three banks as well as your broker to see who has the highest rate.

- Ask how the interest is calculated. Daily, remember, is better than weekly.

- You may get a slightly higher rate at your broker's office because he buys huge certificates of $100,000 or more and then sells you a $1,000 chunk. These jumbo certificates pay higher interest rates than the smaller bank CDs.

- Make certain that the brokerage house will keep track of your CDs and mail you the interest if you like, or reinvest it if that is your wish.

Choosing a CD Interest Rate

Advertising by financial institutions may herald high rates in order to entice you and your money. But before you buy a certificate of deposit from a bank, read the fine print and figure out the interest rate.

- *Compounding.* Note whether the ad says interest is compounded or simple. Compounded is better because it means your interest earns interest. If compounded, is it done annually, semiannually, monthly, daily? It makes a difference. On a one-year certificate of deposit that pays 8 percent simple, interest is just that—8 percent. But when compounded daily, that 8 percent yields the equivalent of 8.33 percent over the course of a year.

- *Floating Rates.* Some accounts and CDs have floating rates in which interest is tied to an index, such as rates on U.S. Treasury securities. Banks should explain the initial rate, and most do, but they cannot tell you what the long-term rate will be, since it fluctuates.

- *Teaser Rates.* Some institutions offer a high introductory rate, which then drops. The high rate is apt to appear in the ads, the low rate in the fine print.

- *Annual Yields.* Often the yield given in an ad is for one year or less, and it assumes upon maturity (all interest rates are quoted on an annual basis) that you will reinvest all the money in another CD paying the same rate. In other words, if you don't roll over your CD, or if you roll it over into an account paying a lower rate, you won't get the advertised yield.

- *To Protect Yourself.* Ask your banker:
  1. What the interest rate will be during the entire life of a fixed rate
  2. What the effective annual yield is
  3. What the penalties are for early withdrawal

- *Highest Yields.* Check the Friday edition of the *Wall Street Journal* for listings of the nation's highest-yielding CDs. If rates are significantly higher out-of-town, call for instructions on purchasing them.

THE 72 RULE

A quick way to calculate how long it will take you to double your investment—at any interest rate—is to use "The 72 Rule."

Divide 72 by the interest rate and you get the number of years it will take to double your money.

For example: 72 divided by 9½ percent is 7.6 years
                  72 divided by 11 percent is 6½ years

Note: "The 72 rule" applies only when interest and dividends are reinvested. It does not take taxes into consideration.

PART THREE
The First $1,000

9
Investing for Income: Bonds

To safeguard your principal and at the same time guarantee long-term income, you can't beat bonds as a sure $1,000 investment.

Bond Basics

Simply stated, a bond (unlike a stock) is an IOU. When you purchase a bond you are, in effect, lending your money to the issuing company or government agency. Bonds come in three types:

1. Those issued by the U.S. Government and its agencies (U.S. Government or Treasury notes and bonds are covered in the next chapter.)

2. Those issued by corporations

3. Those issued by states and municipalities, known as tax-exempt or "munis"

The issuers of the bond are obligated to pay back the full purchase price at a particular time, and not before. This is called the **maturity date.** The reason people buy bonds is to receive a high secure rate of return (called interest) on their investment.

In general, bonds fall into two time-related categories: **intermediate notes,** which mature in two to ten years; and **long-term bonds,** which mature or come due in ten years or longer.

Until your bond matures, you will be receiving a fixed rate of interest on your money. This is called the **coupon rate** and is usually paid out twice a year. For example, on a $1,000 bond that pays 10 percent (fixed rate), you will receive a $50 check every six months until maturity.

You may be interested to know that the term **coupon** dates from the time when all bonds actually came with a page of attached coupons. On each specified date, the owner of the bond clipped off the coupon, took it to the bank, and exchanged it for cash.

The **face value** or denomination of a bond is also known as **par value** and is usually $1,000. That means bonds are sold at $1,000 when they are first issued. After that their price may vary, moving up and down just as stocks do. Depending upon the prevailing market conditions, bonds are sold or traded either **above par** (that is, above $1,000), which is also called **at premium;** or **below par,** which is less than $1,000 and also called **at a discount.**

And, just to make it a bit more confusing, although bonds are issued and sold in $1,000 units, their prices in the newspaper and elsewhere are quoted on the basis of $100, not $1,000. So you must always add a zero to the price. For example, a bond quoted at $105 is really selling for $1,050. (See section entitled "Price and Yield," which follows.)

Buying New or Old Bonds

When buying bonds you can either buy a **new issue,** in which case the issuing company pays the broker's fee; or, you can buy an **older bond** on the open market, in which case *you* pay a commission. New bonds are those issued for the first time to the public. Old bonds are those that someone purchased, held, and then decided to sell before maturity.

After bonds have been issued, *they do not stay at the same price.* They rise and fall in price depending upon supply and demand and upon availability of new bonds that give buyers a higher interest rate or a lower interest rate. If new bonds pay more interest, then older bonds drop in price. If new bonds pay less interest, then older bonds rise in price because they are more desirable.

It is possible to sell your bond before maturity, although the issuer is not obliged to redeem it ahead of time. Investors can almost always sell a bond in the open market through a stockbroker—but it is possible you will not receive what you paid for it, the price being more or less dependent upon the market.

The minimum bond investment is usually $5,000 to $10,000 through brokers. But it is indeed possible to enter the bond market by buying a single $1,000 bond through a stockbroker. You can buy a bond mutual fund or a unit investment trust for $1,000. These vehicles are explained on pages 52–56.

Price and Yield

Just like stock prices, bond prices fluctuate. Their market value changes every day (or several times a day) in reaction to the availability of our number-one commodity: money. As interest rates go up or down, bond prices change. This is due to the fact that the bond coupon or interest rate is set; so the only way the bond market can accommodate to changes in interest rates is by changing the bond's current market price.

It works like this:

- When interest rates go down, bond prices go up.
- When interest rates go up, bond prices fall.

The rule of thumb to keep in mind is: *Bond prices move in exactly the opposite direction from interest rates.*

Let's say you buy a $1,000 bond at 10 percent, which means $100 annually in interest payments. If interest rates move up and the same corporation issues new bonds, it might do so at 10½ percent, or $105 per year. The impact then on the corporation's older bond (the one you own) would be as follows:

- Although its relative value will fall somewhat, the interest, or coupon, rate will remain the same. But the bond's selling price could drop to around $960, where the yield would then approximate 10½ percent. (Yield is the equivalent of 10½ percent on a $1,000 bond, because of the $40 you save by buying the bond for $960.)

Now let's look at the same situation when interest rates fall to 9½ percent. Then the corporation issues new bonds at the lower coupon rate. In this case the older bond (the one you purchased) will rise in value. Thus a 10 percent bond could sell at $105, that is 10 divided by $105 = 9.5 percent.

If you need to raise money and sell your $1,000 bond at $960 and take a $40 loss, someone else may buy it and hold it until maturity, when it will be worth $1,000, making a $40 profit. The total return to that person, including both the interest and the gain in price, is called the **yield to maturity.**

Bonds and the Risk Element

In order to determine a bond's safety, you can consult one of the professional rating services—either Standard & Poor's or Moody's. Their rating books are on the shelves of most public libraries or at your broker's office. The highest rating is triple A. Medium-grade bonds fall into the triple B category, while those that are C or lower are speculative. In general, inexperienced investors should stick with bonds rated A or better.

Moody's		S&P
Aaa	Top quality	AAA
Aa	Excellent	AA
A	Very high	A
Baa	Medium	BBB
Ba	Speculative	BB
B	Lower speculative	B
Caa	Poor & risky	CCC
Ca	Near default	CC
C	In default	C

The two key risk factors are:

- If you must sell before maturity, interest rates may have climbed, making your bond worth less. This has been historically true during inflationary periods.

- Your bonds may be "called in." Most bonds have **call features,** which give the issuer the right to redeem the bond before maturity. The conditions for calling in a bond are given in the statement filed with the SEC when the bonds are first issued to the public.

The call feature is usually not exercised if the current interest rate is the same as or higher than the bond coupon rate. But, if interest rates fall below the bond coupon rate, it is sometimes likely that the bond will be called because now the issuer can borrow money somewhere else at a lower rate. (Remember, a bond is just a loan you make to the issuer, who would naturally prefer to pay the lowest interest rate possible.)

Call Protection

If a bond is called in, you then, of course, lose that steady stream of income you thought you had locked in for a given number of years. But there is a way to protect yourself from calls, and it is especially essential when investing long term. You can buy a bond with "call protection," which guarantees that it will not be called for a specific number of years. Corporate bonds are likely to offer ten-year call protection. Most government bonds are not callable at all.

Who Issues Bonds?

We will cover U.S. Government, or Treasury, bonds and notes in the next chapter, and municipal bonds and corporate bonds here.

Corporate Bonds

Thousands of large U.S. corporations raise money by selling bonds to the public. Some of these companies are small and obscure; others are well known. In general, it is best to stick to the bonds of leading companies, because if you need to sell your bonds to raise cash, you can do so more easily. Look for bonds traded on the New York Stock Exchange. Bond prices and yields are listed in a special section of the newspaper. **Corporate bonds** can be purchased from a stockbroker in $1,000 face value denominations.

Prices for bonds are quoted in the newspaper with fractions listed in eighths. For example, a bond listed at $98¼ is really selling for $982.50. Here's what a typical listing looks like:

Bond	Current Yield	Sales in $1,000	High	Low	Last	Net Change
duPont 8½06	9.1	39	93⅜	92¾	93¼	+⅛

The first column indicates that this E.I. duPont Corporation bond has a coupon rate of 8.5 percent and a maturity date of 2006. In other words, it pays $85 per year for every $1,000 bond. If you divide the coupon rate (8.5 percent) by the current market price (which is listed under "Last" and is $93¼), you will get the current yield (which is 9.1 percent). The volume of bonds traded was 39 bonds. The high was $933.75 and the low $927.75. The closing price was $932.25, up $1.25 per bond.

You may wonder why the yield for this bond rose from 8.5 percent to 9.1 percent. The answer is that the price of the bond has gone down from $1,000, which it was on the first day it was issued, to $930.375.

Are Corporate Bonds for You?

Yes, if you stick with those with top ratings. These could include such well-known corporations as General Motors, Exxon, Xerox, IBM, General Electric, and duPont. But remember, unlike government bonds, corporate bonds are not guaranteed. Your protection is the financial strength of the corporation. And, *the greater the financial strength of the issuer, the lower the coupon or interest rate, because safety is traded off for lower yields.*

CORPORATE BONDS

For Whom

- Anyone seeking high fixed income who also accepts the risk of a changing interest-rate market

Safety Factor

- Can be determined by bond ratings, with AAA and AA being the highest ratings
- Does vary depending upon the corporation
- Are not insured or guaranteed

Minimum Investment

- $1,000

Advantages

- Corporate bonds almost always pay higher interest rates than government bonds or those issued by municipalities.
- You can select bonds to come due when you need your principal repaid.
- Corporate bonds are a good way of investing for income.

Disadvantages

- Many bonds have call provisions.
- There is a lack of liquidity.
- Interest income is subject to federal, state, and local taxes.
- There is generally no appreciation of principal as there is with stocks.

Hint: Unless you are experienced, you are better off playing with corporate bonds through a corporate bond mutual fund or unit trust because the bonds are professionally selected and managed (see pages 52–56).

Municipal Bonds

Municipal bonds survived the wide-reaching effects of the 1986 Tax Reform Act and remain desirable for those investors in the 28 percent tax bracket seeking interest income that is exempt from federal taxation.

By far the largest number of bonds offered are tax-exempt or municipal bonds. These are issued by cities, counties, states, and special agencies to finance various projects. Their biggest plus: Interest paid is exempt from federal income tax and state and local taxes in the area where issued. (If, however, you buy municipals of another state, they will be subject to taxes in your state.) Because of the tax advantage, municipal bonds pay lower interest rates than comparable corporate bonds or government securities. Your interest and principal are repaid to you by taxes and revenues collected by the municipalities issuing the bonds.

Municipal bond dealers and the major retail brokers such as Merrill Lynch, Shearson Lehman Hutton, or Prudential Bache are interested in working only with customers who have a minimum of $25,000 to invest in these bonds. Smaller investors, however, can participate through purchasing unit investment trusts or municipal bond funds, which are explained on pages 53–56.

How to Select Tax-Exempts

There are three factors to check when considering tax-exempt bonds: *safety, yield,* and *liquidity.* You can check the safety of any bond, tax-exempt or not, through Moody's or Standard & Poor's rating services. In addition to sticking to A-rated bonds, you can increase your safety factor by:

- Buying bonds that come with a federal government guarantee
- Buying bonds that are insured

There are several private concerns that insure bonds, among them the American Municipal Bond Assurance Corporation and Municipal Bond Assurance Association. Because there have been a few cases of municipal bonds that have defaulted (the best-known example being the Washington Public Power System), insured bonds are a sound idea.

In order to insure a bond, the issuer pays an insurance premium that ranges from 0.1 percent to 2 percent of total principal and interest. The insurance company then agrees to pay both the principal and the interest to bondholders if the issuer defaults. Policies generally last the life of the bond. You will find that insured bonds have slightly lower yields, for obvious reasons. For additional information on insured municipal bonds, write to:

Municipal Bond Assurance Corporation
1 State Street Plaza
New York, NY 10004

The second factor in municipal bond selection is *yield*. Tax-exempts, as we mentioned before, pay lower interest rates than most taxable bonds and therefore are not appropriate for people in low tax brackets or for placement in already tax-deferred retirement accounts.

The third factor involved in municipal bond selection is *liquidity*; that is, the ability to find someone who wants to buy your bond. It is best to stick with bonds of large, well-known municipalities or state governments. If you want to sell an obligation of the Moorland, Iowa, School District, it may be weeks before you find a dealer willing to buy these obscure bonds.

You can also avoid the liquidity problem by buying a tax-exempt unit trust or a bond mutual fund.

The Tax Law & Municipals

While the 1986 tax reform curtailed or wiped out most shelters, it left munis as one of the few ways to earn tax-free income. Yet the reform did entail changes in munis you should know about.

First, it **reduced the number as well as the type of tax-free bonds** that state and local governments can issue. Since interest on munis is exempt from federal tax, by restricting the number of tax-exempt bonds available, the Fed hopes to channel bond buyers' money into taxable bonds, enabling it to collect more in taxes.

General obligation bonds, sold to help build roads, schools, and government buildings, are tax-exempt as long as no more than 10 percent of their proceeds goes to a private enterprise. Bonds issued for non-profit organizations also are tax-exempt. GOs have the highest safety ratings.

Industrial development bonds are issued to finance facilities that are in turn leased to private corporations. The tax law stipulates that if more than 10 percent of the proceeds raised by their sale is used by private enterprise, the interest a bondholder receives may be subject to a special tax, known as the alternative minimum tax (AMT). The AMT is designed to make sure that Americans with tax-sheltered investments do not escape paying income taxes. Before investing in an

51

industrial development bond, check with your accountant to see if you are subject to the AMT; if so, avoid these particular bonds.

Second, **no longer are municipalities allowed to issue tax-exempt bonds for so-called "nonessential purposes":** for pollution control facilities, sports complexes, convention halls, parking facilities, etc. Most issues remain exempt from state and local taxes where issued but are fully subject to federal tax.

Although the sharp reduction in income tax rates makes tax-exempt income less advantageous than before, munis continue to have justified appeal: If, for example, you are married, file a joint return, and earn $45,000 annually, you need a yield of 10.76 percent on a taxable investment to equal a 7.75 percent tax-exempt yield. And, keep in mind that while interest on CDs and corporate bonds is subject to federal and state taxes, and interest on Treasuries to federal tax, *interest on many municipals is free from city, state, and local taxes.* These triple-exempt bonds are especially good for people living in states with high income taxes.

Hint: Zero coupon municipals (see page 57) are an excellent way to save for a child's education. They are sold at a discount and redeemed in the future at a higher face value. And you never have to pay federal income tax on them.

Bond Mutual Funds

The bond investor with only $1,000 can buy into a bond fund or unit investment trust, in which risk is spread out through participation in large, diversified portfolios of bonds that are professionally selected. There are two types of bond funds: **open-ended managed bond mutual funds** and **closed-end unit investment trusts.** You need to know about both.

The Managed Bond Mutual Fund

If you have $1,000 to $5,000 and want the advantages of diversification and professional management, you should consider this type of fund. As is the case with any other mutual fund, in a bond fund you purchase shares of a professionally managed portfolio. The manager periodically reviews the contents of the fund's portfolio and makes buy-and-sell decisions based on performance and market conditions. The value of the fund's portfolio fluctuates—it is *not* fixed. Most funds have a minimum investment requirement of $1,000 and offer both convenience and diversification. Interest is automatically reinvested unless you give directions to the contrary; and an increasing number of bond funds allow you to write checks, usually a minimum of $500, against the value of your shares.

Bond funds come in two varieties: **load funds** and **no-load funds.** Those with a load are sold through stockbrokers and have a sales charge of as much as 8 percent of your initial investment. No-load funds are bought directly from the fund and are free of a sales charge. Since there is no proven difference in performance between a load and no-load fund, you might as well buy shares in a no-load fund.

If you ever wish to sell, the fund will buy back your shares at the current market price, which could be more or less than what you originally paid.

Tax-Exempt Unit Investment Trusts

For those who wish to lock in a fixed tax-exempt yield, a **unit investment trust** is ideal. This also requires a minimum investment of $1,000 per unit. These are set up by big brokerage houses and bond dealers who buy several million dollars' worth of bonds and then sell them to individual investors in $1,000 pieces. You pay the broker a one-time fixed fee, about 7 percent to 8 percent of the value of the units.

Unit trusts are prepackaged, diversified portfolios of tax-exempt bonds that lock in a specific, unchanging yield. Unlike bond mutual funds, they are "unmanaged": they are "closed-end" trusts—in other words, once the bonds for the trust have been selected, no new issues are added—ever. (Issues that turn out to be a problem, however, can be sold in order to minimize losses.) The trust gradually liquidates itself as the bonds mature; until then, the unit price (but not the interest rate) fluctuates with prevailing interest rates.

When you buy a unit trust, you are buying a share of a larger portfolio. This has the advantage of reducing your risk through diversification—by spreading out your investment dollars over twenty or thirty bonds. A trust has the added plus of professional selection. The average investor does not have time to sort through hundreds of bond prospectuses and then check each one's credit rating. The bond trust does this for you (so does the bond mutual fund).

Nevertheless, neither diversification nor professional management completely erases the risk factor. Bond prices fall when interest rates rise and rise when interest rates fall; so will unit trust prices rise and fall with changes in interest rates.

The concept behind the unit investment trust is that if you hold on to it until maturity, you will then get back your initial investment. Maturity can be ten, twenty, or even thirty-plus years, depending on the trust. In the interim, you will receive a fixed amount of tax-free income, usually on a monthly basis.

Hint: Don't be surprised if your checks are not the same every month. As bonds mature or are called, this activity is reflected in your monthly checks. This monthly fluctuation does not reduce the amount you receive upon the trust's maturity.

If you do not wish to hold the trust until maturity, you can sell it at any time in a "secondary market" either to the sponsor or to another broker. What you get back will depend on the market. If interest rates have fallen, you will get more; but if they've gone up, it's possible that you may not even get back your original price.

Talk to your broker in order to find out which trusts are available now, and at what price. Be certain to check the rating of the bonds held in the trust. If you're conservative, stick with AAA-rated bonds, or buy an insured trust.

Trusts are ideal for those investors who wish to spend less than $25,000. They offer the investor with a limited amount of money a way to get into the action at an affordable price and hold a diversified portfolio.

Single-State Investments Trusts

The best unit trust is often a **single-state investment trust.** It contains bonds that have a triple tax exemption—that is, they are free from federal, state, and local taxes for residents of that state. You can buy them from regional brokers, large brokerage firms, and bond specialists. They contain portfolios of tax-free bonds issued for a variety of public purposes within a single state.

In addition to the large brokerage houses, there are several companies that sponsor single-state trusts. You can contact them for further information. These include:

- John Nuveen & Company, which regularly issues new single-state trusts. Its Multi-State Trust Series is available in Arizona, California, Colorado, Connecticut, Florida, Georgia, Maryland, Massachusetts, Michigan, Minnesota, New Jersey, New York, North Carolina, Ohio, Pennsylvania, Texas, and Virginia. (The Municipal Investment Trust Funds, which have triple-exempt unit trusts for residents of New York, California, Pennsylvania, Maryland, Minnesota, and Michigan, are cosponsored by Merrill Lynch, Dean Witter, Shearson Lehman Hutton, and Prudential Bache. Contact the local office of any one of these brokers.) For additional data contact:

> John Nuveen & Company
> 140 Broadway
> New York, NY 10005
> 212-208-2300

> or

> 333 W. Wacker Drive
> Chicago, IL 60606
> 312-917-7700

• Van Kampen Merritt offers a variety of triple-exempt trusts:
> Van Kampen Merritt
> 2 Penn Plaza
> Philadelphia, PA 19102
> 800-523-4556
> 215-972-0555

Tax-Exempt Bond Mutual Funds

The investor seeking tax-exempt income has an alternative to the closed-end exempt unit trust: **managed mutual funds.** The entire portfolio is made up of tax-exempt municipal bonds. They are available for a minimum investment of $1,000 and operate like any other managed mutual fund—that is, the management buys and sells securities in order to maximize the fund's yield. Unlike a unit investment trust where the yield is fixed, these funds' shares fluctuate on a daily basis.

Find your tax bracket on the left, then at the top of the table find the tax-exempt yield. Read down to determine what yield you need on a taxable security to equal the yield on a municipal.

Tax Bracket	6.5%	7%	7.5%	8%
15%	7.64	8.23	8.82	9.41
28%	9.02	9.72	10.41	11.11
33%	9.70	10.45	11.19	11.94

TAX-EXEMPT UNIT TRUST vs. TAX-EXEMPT BOND MUTUAL FUND

Here's how to determine which one is for you:

- In a tax-exempt unit trust the basic investment is fixed; no trading activity is conducted after initial bond purchases are made by the trust.

- In a tax-exempt bond fund, investments are bought and sold in order to maximize a high tax-exempt income.

- Sometimes bond funds perform better than fixed trusts, and vice versa.

- Unit trust sponsors take most of their fee up front when you buy. It ranges up to 8 percent of your purchase.

- Many, but not all, bond funds do not charge the investor a fee for buying or selling shares. They are called no-load or no-fee funds.

- Unit investment trusts are intended to be held to maturity, typically 5 to 30 years.

- Bond mutual funds can be for long- or short-term holding.

- Unit trusts provide regular income checks.

- Bond funds provide income when you sell your shares.

Before you buy any municipal bond mutual fund or unit trust, take time to read the prospectus. Know what securities it contains, what their ratings are, and when you will receive your interest or dividend payments. Check out the various fees and charges, too. Don't leave yourself open for any hidden surprises.

Zero Coupon Bonds

If you will need money for college tuition, retirement, or to meet some other long-term financial goal, **zero coupon bonds** offer a viable solution, because you make a small investment today and get a large balloon payment in the future.

A "zero," unlike regular bonds, pays zero interest until maturity. To compensate for this fact, it is sold at a deep discount, well below the $1,000 standard bond price, and it increases in value at a compound rate so that by maturity it is worth much more than when you bought it. Although this type of bond does not pay interest along the way, you will be taxed annually by the IRS as though it did, because the government wants to collect the tax due along the way.

Here's an example of a recent zero: A $1,000 zero that yields 11.9 percent and matures in twenty years will sell for only $85.40. In other words, you invest $85.40 at 11.9 percent today. 11.9 percent interest is paid on your investment and the reinvested interest, and after twenty years your $85.40 will equal $1,000. Interest "turns into" principal, and is paid to you in a lump sum upon maturity.

As you can see, with a zero coupon bond you know ahead of time exactly how much money you will have when the bond comes due. Yet because zeros, unlike regular bonds, lock in interest, you get a slightly lower yield, about ½ to 1 percentage point below bonds that have a regular coupon. (See page 44 for an explanation of coupons.)

There are four types of zeros.

1. *Corporate zeros* are issued by large corporations. The very first zero, in fact, was issued by J.C. Penney in 1981. Offered at $250 each, they mature in 1992, when they will be worth $1,000. That works out to a 13.5 percent yield. Because they are a long-term investment, you need to have faith in the corporation and its credit worthiness. There are very few corporate zeros.

2. *Treasury zeros* are packaged and sold by large brokerage and investment houses. These institutions buy huge lots of long-term U.S. Treasury bonds, clip off (or "strip off") the semiannual interest coupons, then sell these coupons, which come due twice a year during the life of the bond. Each package guarantees that the buyer of these coupons will get $1,000 upon maturity. Principal and interest are guaranteed by the U.S. Government. These "strip bonds," as they are called, are also known by various names: Merrill Lynch sells TIGERs, which stands for Treasury Investment Growth Receipt; Salomon Brothers' CATS are Certificates of Accrual on Treasury Securities and are available through Prudential-Bache; and LIONs, Lehman Investment Opportunity Notes, are sold through Shearson Lehman Hutton.

Recent examples:
1. A six-year Treasury zero yielding 11.38 percent sold for $474.
2. A twelve-year zero yielding 11.42 percent sold for $342.
3. An eighteen-year zero yielding 11.07 percent sold for $132.

3. *Tax-exempt zeros* are issued by municipalities, states, and other agencies. Just as with other municipal bonds, their interest is exempt from federal income tax and from state and local tax in the issuing community. Like other tax-exempt bonds, they pay a lower rate.

4. *Zero coupon CDs* are similar to zero coupon bonds. They are obligations of large banks and, like bank deposits, are insured up to $100,000 by the FDIC.

ZERO COUPON BONDS

For Whom

- Those who know they will need a certain amount of money at a certain time in the future
- Those who can hold bonds until maturity because zero prices fluctuate widely

Minimum

- Varies; never less than $100

Safety Factor

- Minimal risk

Advantages

- You know precisely how much you must invest now to get a certain amount of money on a certain date in the future.

- You do not have to be concerned with the reinvestment of interest payments as is the case with regular bonds.

Disadvantages

- When interest rates rise, the value of the zeros you hold falls even more than the value of regular bonds, because, since you have no cash in hand from interest payments, you cannot take a zero's interest and reinvest it at a higher rate elsewhere.

- Yields are ½ to 1 percentage point below ordinary bonds.

- The IRS insists that taxes be paid annually on zero coupon bonds just as if you actually received the interest.

- You are paying taxes on theoretical interest even though no cash is received until the date of maturity. The buyer of a regular bond pays taxes too, but also receives interest payments in the form of cash twice a year.

Hint: If you do not want to get locked into the lower yield of a longer-term zero coupon bond because you fear inflation and the higher interest rates it brings, buy zeros with shorter maturities.

HOW TO BUILD A COLLEGE FUND WITH ZEROS

Recently a grandmother attending the first birthday celebration of her granddaughter announced a gift of $10,000 toward the little girl's college education, which would start in 2008. Her cost for this $10,000 was only $1,060, because she had purchased zero coupon bonds from her broker that were due to mature then.

You, too, can use zero coupon bonds to prepare for the day when your child or grandchild goes to college.

- Select zeros scheduled to come due at the right time.

- You can set up a custodial account through your broker or bank. This type of account holds money, stocks, or bonds in a parent's name for the child until he or she is of age. Investment interest in excess of $1,000 on gifts to children is taxed at the parent's tax bracket if the child is under 14.

- Gifts made by grandparents and relatives other than parents are taxed at the child's (presumably) lower rate, regardless of the child's age.

10
U.S. Treasury Notes & Bonds

When you have accumulated an extra $1,000 or more, it's time to consider one of the safest of all investment vehicles—**Treasuries,** which is Wall Street-ese for securities issued by the U.S. Government. Long regarded as an ideal place for a portion of anyone's savings, these investments have three things in their favor:

- They are the safest form of investment because the U.S. Government guarantees to pay you back.
- They are extremely liquid and can be sold at any time.
- Interest earned is exempt from state and local taxes.

Where do Treasuries come from? Uncle Sam constantly borrows money, not only to finance building battleships but also to cover the high federal deficit, by issuing short-term Treasury bills and longer-term notes and bonds. (The difference among all three—bills, notes, and bonds—is the time limit or maturity. They run from a minimum of thirteen weeks to a maximum of thirty years.)

- **Treasury bills** mature in a year or less. They come in 13-, 26-, and 52-week maturities and require a minimum investment of $10,000. Instead of paying interest, they are sold below face value—that is, at a discount.
- **Treasury notes** mature in two to ten years and require a minimum investment of $5,000 for those maturing in less than four years, and $1,000 for those maturing in more than four years.
- **Treasury bonds** mature in ten years or more; the minimum investment is $1,000.

interest – yield relationship?

So, for the highest safety rating you generally must accept a comparatively low interest rate; however, since the government has to finance a huge deficit yields are relatively high.

Most corporate and municipal bonds have a call feature (see page 47). This means that the issuer has the privilege of redeeming the bonds prior to maturity. In other words, issuers of bonds have a right to "call" in or redeem a bond at a specific date for cash. Redemption prices are determined and the call year stated when the bond is initially offered to the public. All Treasury notes and most Treasury bonds are not callable. This is an advantage of Treasuries in addition to their safety and exemption from state and local taxes.

What About Yields?

Yields on Treasuries vary, depending upon the supply and demand of money. This means that when money is tight the yield will tend to be higher than when it's more readily available. When you invest in a Treasury you must realize that you won't know the precise yield until it is set at auction. These public auctions are held periodically by the U.S. Treasury for major banks and government bond dealers. The public may also participate (we will tell you how in a bit).

Both notes and bonds have a "par" value of 100, which means 100 percent of the face amount—$1,000. Although the interest rate is fixed and set by the Treasury auction, notes and bonds can sell above par or below par, that is, above $1,000 or below $1,000.

If they sell above par, you will pay a premium, and the effective yield will be less than the interest rate printed on the bond. For example, if you buy a 10 percent bond and you pay $1,030 you are paying above par, or at a premium.

$$\frac{\begin{array}{c}\text{10 percent}\\\text{(the interest rate printed on the bond)}\end{array}}{\begin{array}{c}\$1,030\\\text{(the price you paid for a \$1,000 bond)}\end{array}} = \begin{array}{c}\text{9.7 percent}\\\text{(the effective yield)}\end{array}$$

Treasuries also have a **coupon rate,** a term left over from the days when bonds had an attached page of coupons; on the set date the owner of the bond clipped the coupon and took it to the bank to exchange for the interest earned in cash.

If the bond sells below par, it is selling at a discount, and the effective yield will be higher than the coupon rate. For example, if you buy a 10 percent bond and you pay $970, then you're buying it at a discount or below par.

$$\frac{\text{10 percent}}{\$970} = \text{an effective yield of 10.3 percent}$$

How to Become Part of the Auction

You can buy Treasuries through a broker or your bank for $25 to $35 per bond. But there's no need to pay a commission, because you can also buy them through the mail or in person from the Federal Reserve Bank in your area, or the Bureau of Public Debt. (There are twelve Federal Reserve districts, each with a main bank and thirty-seven additional branches.) When the U.S. Treasury holds an auction in which large banks and government bond dealers bid for notes, bills, and bonds, their bids are actually placed through the Federal Reserve banking system (see list on page 65).

Auctions for Treasuries are announced. The *Wall Street Journal* and other newspapers provide this material, or you can call your district Federal Reserve office and get a copy of their newsletter, *Highlights of Treasury Offerings,* which contains a list of auction dates.

The auctions have a regular schedule for the most part. In general:

- 13- and 26-week bills are auctioned every Monday.
- 52-week bills are auctioned once a month.
- 2-year notes are auctioned once a month.
- 3-year and longer notes are auctioned every three months.
- Bonds are auctioned every three months.

Bidding

The U.S. Treasury sells its securities to the public through the Federal Reserve System at periodic auctions on both a competitive and a noncompetitive basis. Competitive sales are made almost entirely to professional traders and institutions. These "big guns," such as banks, mutual funds, and pension funds, state the yields at which they would be willing to buy the Treasury's issue. The average individual, however, should enter a noncompetitive bid. In this type of bid, you simply order securities without stating a yield. Your request is then filled at the average of all the accepted competitive bids. (*Note:* Bids are in yields, not price.)

You can easily enter a noncompetitive bid by mail. If you do so, your bid must be postmarked no later than the day before the auction and received on or before the auction date.

You can also go in person to the nearest Federal Reserve office with your bid by 1 P.M. Eastern time on the day of the auction and make your purchase there. Arrive early, however, as lines can be long, especially when interest rates are high.

Regardless of whether you buy in person or through the mail, you must fill out an order form, known as a tender. This one-page form is available from all Federal Reserve Banks and their branches. On the form there's a place to check the type of bid you wish to make: competitive or noncompetitive. You'll also need to fill in your name, address, and Social Security number, as well as a telephone number where you can be reached during the day.

You can pay with cash, a cashier's check, or a certified personal check. Make certain the check is payable to the specific Federal Reserve Bank from which you are purchasing your Treasury security.

Finally, you must fill in information that enables the interest and principal payments from the Treasuries you are buying to be deposited directly into your bank or financial institution. You will see a line for "routing number." This is simply the nine-digit number that appears on the lower left of your personal check. Next comes the name of the financial institution to which payments will be made, your account number at that institution, the type of account (savings, checking, etc.), and the name of the account holder.

Sign the form, date it, and submit it to the Federal Reserve Bank or branch in your area, or, if you live in the Washington, DC, area, to the Bureau of Public Debt.

Treasury Direct System

All sales of Treasuries are recorded on a book-entry basis electronically through what is called the Treasury Direct System. You do not receive a certificate as was the case in the past before the age of the computer. The Treasury Direct System is designed for investors who plan to hold their securities until maturity. If you need to sell before maturity, you must transfer your Treasuries out of the Treasury Direct System into the commercial book-entry system. To do this, set up an account with a stockbroker or a bank that will sell them for you, for a fee. To transfer your notes or bonds, fill out Form PD179, "Security Transfer Request," available from any Federal Reserve Bank or branch.

Hint: If you know you will not be holding your Treasuries until they mature, buy them from a broker or bank. This automatically puts you in the commercial book-entry system from the beginning.

After the Auction

Using Your Broker

After the auction is over you can buy and sell Treasury notes, bonds, and bills through your broker in what is known as the secondary market. That is, Treasuries are continually bought and sold after they are first issued.

If you have an account at a brokerage house, your broker will act as your purchasing agent. Regular commissions are charged on orders. The broker's fee will vary from firm to firm, ranging from $25 to $35 or more for orders of any size. Some brokers charge a flat fee—maybe $50, $75, or $100, regardless of the size of the order. Most brokers buy Treasuries primarily as a service to their clients, because they do not make much on the transaction.

Many discount brokers will also buy Treasuries. It is worth calling several in your area because the cost to you will be much lower than with a full-service broker.

THE TWELVE FEDERAL RESERVE BANKS

Boston
600 Atlantic Avenue
Boston, MA 02106
617-973-3800

New York
33 Liberty Street
New York, NY 10045
212-720-6619

Richmond
701 East Byrd Street
Richmond, VA 23219
804-697-8000

Philadelphia
100 North Sixth Street
Philadelphia, PA 19105
215-574-6580

Cleveland
1455 East Sixth Street
Cleveland, OH 44101
216-579-2490

Atlanta
104 Marietta Street NW
Atlanta, GA 30301
404-521-8653

Chicago
230 South La Salle Street
Chicago, IL 60690
312-786-1110

Minneapolis
250 Marquette Avenue
Minneapolis, MN 55480
612-340-2051

Dallas
400 South Akard Street
Dallas, TX 75222
214-651-6177

Kansas
925 Grand Avenue
Kansas City, MO 64198
816-881-2409

St. Louis
411 Locust Street
St. Louis, MO 63166
314-444-8444

San Francisco
San Francisco, CA 94120
415-974-2330

U.S. TREASURIES

For Whom

- Investors seeking absolute safety

- Those with a minimum of $1,000

- Those who enjoy helping Uncle Sam

Fee

- There is no fee if ordered directly from the Federal Reserve.

- Banks and brokers charge various fees, ranging from a few dollars to as high as $50 or $75.

Safety Factor

- The highest possible

- Backed by the U.S. Government

Advantages

- Principal and interest are guaranteed against default.

- You can sell Treasuries through a broker before maturity without loss because interest accrues daily until date of your sale.

- Maximum liquidity

- The state and local tax exemption makes Treasuries especially attractive for those who live in a state with high taxes.

Disadvantages

- Troublesome to purchase unless you pay the fee and use your bank or broker.

- Competitive bidding on Treasuries is a skilled art and should not be attempted by the average investor.

- Since you have to pay the Treasury in advance of the auction, you will lose some interest if your money was in an interest-bearing account.

- Buying a bank CD is easier, generally pays about the same interest or a little less, but interest on a CD is fully taxable.

TREASURY TELEPHONE HELP

Call: 202-287-4113 A recorded message with general information on how to order Treasuries by mail and a listing of other important data and telephone numbers. At the end of the recorded announcement, an analyst will answer your specific questions.

Most of the Federal Reserve Banks listed in this chapter have recorded announcements with similar details. Pamphlets and other material on Treasuries are available from: Bureau of the Public Debt, Dept. F, Washington, DC 20239-1200.

You may also be interested in the following publications:

Basic Information on Treasury Bills (free)
Federal Reserve Bank of New York
Public Information Department
33 Liberty Street
New York, NY 10045
212-720-6130

Buying Treasury Securities at Federal Reserve Banks ($4.50)
Federal Reserve Bank of Richmond
Public Services Department
P.O. Box 27471
Richmond, VA 23262
804-697-8000

U.S. Financial Data ($18/year; weekly newsletter)
Federal Reserve Bank of St. Louis
P.O. Box 66953
St. Louis, MO 63166
314-444-8660

Grant's Interest Rate Observer ($375/year; semimonthly)
233 Broadway
Suite 4008
New York, NY 10279
212-608-7994

11
Public Utility Company Stocks

What Is a Stock?

A stock represents part ownership in a company, and anyone who owns a stock is called a stockholder or shareholder. When a company wants to raise capital to expand, it can borrow the money from the bank or it can issue, or sell, stocks and bonds to the public. (See Chapter 9 on bonds).

In order to document the fact that people purchase stock, the company issues a stock certificate to each shareholder. This piece of paper shows the number of shares owned by that person.

If the company is profitable, the owners of common stock share in the profits in two ways: They gain income through **dividends** and dividend increases, and they benefit as the stock increases in price, known as **appreciation.** A dividend is a periodic payment made from a company's earnings to stockholders. Most dividends are paid four times a year. The board of directors can increase, decrease, or even cancel dividends, depending on the company's profits. Dividend payments vary from stock to stock. In fact, some companies never pay dividends. Those that consistently pay dividends are known as **income stocks** and investors buy them precisely because they want the steady cash payments. This is the case with public utility stocks. The stocks of companies that pay little or no dividends are known as **growth stocks.** Investors buy them because they expect the price of the stock to grow over time. Growth stocks, which are riskier than income stocks, are discussed in Chapter 17.

You may buy stock in any publicly held corporation—one whose shares are traded publicly. (Many U.S. companies are privately held and do not sell shares to the public.) In addition to individuals, institutions also buy stocks. **Institutional investors** include employee pension funds and mutual funds.

Stocks are sold to the public in two steps: Initially, stocks are sold in the **primary market**; thereafter, these same stocks are resold to other investors through a stock exchange in what is called the **secondary market.** The secondary market is not any one place but includes the New York, American, and regional stock exchanges as well as the over-the-counter market. These exchanges are marketplaces where certain qualified stocks approved by the exchange are listed for buying and selling. The exchanges do not own the stocks nor do they influence the price. They merely function as an auction place. Although the price of a stock is fixed when it is initially offered for sale to the public, its price continually fluctuates thereafter, depending on the interest of buyers and sellers at any one time.

Stocks of public utility companies have traditionally been sound, high-yielding investments and as such are considered safe enough for "widows and orphans." Because of their generally solid dividends and high safety ranking, you can invest at the $1,000 level, even though other common stocks are better purchased with investments of $5,000 or more. In general, of course, the greater the risk element in an investment, the more money you should have to cushion any losses.

And utilities are also appealing because of their dividend reinvestment plans (see pages 18–19). Some utilities even offer a 5 percent discount when shares are bought through these plans.

Gas, light, and water companies are rarely subject to competition; in fact, they are usually monopolies. Even in a recession, everybody needs and uses the services they provide.

Finding Bright Lights

Begin in your own backyard:

Step 1

Call the investor or public relations department of your nearest utility company for a copy of the annual report. Take a look through it to see whether:

- Earnings per share are rising
- Dividends are increasing
- Plant construction is completed
- The area's population is growing
- The company is facing any lawsuits

Step 2

Track the company's stock price for several weeks by looking in the newspaper; be alert to trends up or down. Avoid buying shares at their 52-week high. (See page 98 for how to read stock market tables.)

Step 3

Call a local stockbroker for an investment opinion and research report. You can do this whether or not you have an account.

Step 4

Compare the brokerage firm's report with that in *Value Line Investment Survey* or Standard & Poor's *Stock Reports.* These two key reference books are available at most public libraries and brokerage offices. *Value Line* ranks stocks for safety; stick with those with a #1 or #2 ranking.

Step 5

Read any press coverage of the company's prospects or problems.

Step 6

If you decide to buy shares, do so through a discount broker to save on commissions and sign up for the company's dividend reinvestment plan, if it has one.

PART FOUR

The First $2,000

12
Your IRA and/or Keogh Plan

Without a doubt, the very first $2,000 that you manage to accumulate should be invested in an **IRA** (individual retirement account) or in a **Keogh plan.** An IRA, just as its name implies, is a tax-advantaged account into which individuals contribute money that is invested for their retirement. A Keogh plan is a similar tax-advantaged account designed for those who are self-employed. The money invested grows free of taxes until it is taken out. That means interest and dividend income accumulates on a tax-deferred basis.

Life expectancy for an American baby born today is well over 70 years. That means most of us will eventually spend some time in retirement, so it goes without saying that preparing for the years when we're not working has become an absolute necessity unless we want to face melted cheese and tuna casseroles for dinner day in and day out during our golden years.

With very few exceptions, every American should have an IRA, Keogh, or **401(k) plan,** or, if possible, all three. (A 401(k) plan is one in which your company deducts a certain amount from your salary upon your request and puts it into a retirement account. It is also known as a salary-reduction plan.)

These may sound like stodgy ways to save, but the tax breaks offered by each of these three plans make saving very worthwhile; and fairly flexible rules provide a wide array of places to put your money, known to Wall Streeters as "investment vehicles." These vehicles include stocks, bonds, real estate, mutual funds, and Treasury issues. In fact, few things in the financial world are as powerful and helpful as an IRA. According to investment advisors Scudder, Stevens and Clark, if at age 25 you start to save $2,000 a year in an IRA yielding only 5 percent a year, you will accumulate $242,000 by age 65. At an annual rate of 10 percent, that amount would grow to $885,000. So fund your IRA starting today!

WHAT YOU WILL HAVE WHEN YOU ARE 65

Age when start saving $2,000 per year in an IRA	Annual rate of return		
	5%	10%	15%
25	$242,000	$885,000	$3,558,000
35	133,000	329,000	869,000
45	66,000	115,000	205,000
55	25,000	32,000	41,000

What an IRA Is

What exactly is an IRA? It's an "individual retirement account" designed to help you save for the day when you or your spouse is no longer working. Legally, there is no official minimum for opening an IRA, but most plans require at least $250, and the benefits tend to be greater at that level: Interest rates are higher, compounding is more generous, and there are more investment choices open to you with $250.

Anyone who is working can put up to 100 percent of the first $2,000 he or she earns annually into an IRA every year. If you earn less than

$2,000 a year—let's say $1,275—you could contribute that entire amount. But even if you're a rock star making millions of dollars every year, $2,000 is still the maximum you can contribute annually.

Although there is a maximum yearly contribution of $2,000, the account increases in value through the interest earned or the dividends paid out. These additional dollars stay in the account along with whatever you contribute, until you retire and begin withdrawing your money.

If both husband and wife are working, each can contribute $2,000 to separate accounts every year and take $4,000 off their joint income tax return. If one spouse does not work, then the working spouse can contribute up to $2,250. Note that in this "spousal account," however, some portion of the money must be set aside in each spouse's name; it need not be equal amounts.

Whether you're inclined to be conservative or speculative, there's an investment program that's right for your retirement plan. The various choices are explained in this chapter.

First, let's look at some of the very convincing arguments for opening an IRA:

- There are tax benefits for all who open an IRA or Keogh plan. Taxpayers not part of a qualified pension plan can deduct up to $2,000 a year from pre-tax earnings. And, whether you have a qualified pension plan or not, returns earned in an IRA aren't taxed until withdrawn.

- The recent turmoil over the financial well-being of the Social Security system has, or should have, alerted everyone to the fact that it can no longer be counted on as basic income for retirement. Even government-supported medical benefits have been tightened, reducing the portion of a retiree's bill covered by the system. You should regard Social Security only as a means for covering subsistence-level items. At most, Social Security benefits replace only 28 percent of salary for someone earning $35,000 or more upon retirement.

- Companies are getting wise, too, and are not always inclined to be any more generous than they have to be. Pension plans are trending downward, and benefits are generally being reduced.

- Bailouts have been necessary to rescue the Social Security system, railroad, and other large federal retirement systems. And other private retirement systems consistently come under the gun as programs teeter under the weight of huge payments to beneficiaries. Keep in mind, too, that more and more companies are tapping pension coffers to raise dollars for expansion, mergers, etc. During the past several years, over 135 companies actually closed out their retirement plans. Many substituted less expensive programs.

Where to Invest It

Several **custodians** are officially approved as places to set up IRAs. The most popular are banks, brokerage firms, and mutual funds. Consider all three before opening your account, taking into consideration how much money you have, your interest in monitoring your account, and your appetite for risk.

Deciding where to put your IRA and Keogh dollars is very much related to personal temperament as well as market timing. If you tend to be cautious, or if you're nervous watching the stock market go up and down, then a bank CD is probably your best bet. But if you enjoy playing the market and are astute in selecting stocks, consider putting your IRA with a broker.

Age, too, should play a role in your choice of custodian. Investors near retirement should be more conservative than those in their twenties. Fixed-income securities rather than speculative-growth stocks are a more logical choice.

Here is a thumbnail sketch of your custodian choices. Remember that although you can divide your IRA contributions into as many investment choices as you like (as long as you stay within the dollar limitations), it's best to keep those choices to a reasonable number. It's difficult to keep track of too many plans and to continually make that many investment decisions.

Banks
The safest and probably the most convenient choice for an IRA is a bank **CD** or certificate of deposit. It is insured up to $100,000 and interest rates are guaranteed for the entire investment period, that is, until the CD matures.

Most banks, savings and loans, and credit unions charge little or nothing to set up and maintain an IRA. But don't count on it—some do indeed have monthly maintenance charges. That means, as in every institutional transaction, you absolutely must read the fine print carefully.

Bank CDs pay whatever rate of interest the bank wants, and these rates vary considerably among individual banks/institutions. Most have fixed interest rates, while others have variable rates that float up and down with general interest rates. Most banks require a $250 or $500 minimum to open a CD for an IRA. Bank CDs range in length from several months to several years. Think carefully before deciding how long a term CD to buy. Remember: There's a risk involved in buying a long-term CD, say one that matures or comes due in five years, because rates may go up during that five-year period, thus making your original investment, with its locked-in interest rate, less attractive than newer, higher-yielding CDs. The shorter the CD's time period, the more conservative your play. It is true you are at a disadvantage if rates fall, but if you lock in a long-term rate, you eliminate the chance of taking advantage of rising interest rates.

Mutual Funds

The inner workings of **mutual funds** are explained in great detail in Chapters 9 and 15. But as far as the pros and cons of using one for your IRA or Keogh plan are concerned, here is what you should know.

Just about all mutual funds—which are companies that pool money together from individuals in order to buy a wide variety of stocks, bonds, and nearly anything else—offer IRAs. Even though you can find a mutual fund specializing in gold or foreign stocks, your own good judgment should steer you in more sane directions. Remember—you're saving for your own retirement.

Look for mutual funds that invest in money market funds, common stocks selected for appreciation, and bonds aimed at high current income.

Avoid speculative stocks, commodities, hedge funds, gold and precious metals, and foreign funds. And steer clear of funds that are already tax exempt. Since IRAs are sheltered from taxes, you don't need that feature. Also, tax-exempt funds tend to pay a slightly lower return than taxable funds.

How do mutual funds compare with bank CDs for your IRA or Keogh?

A MUTUAL FUND FOR YOUR IRA?

Pros	Cons
■ Potential for substantial gains	■ Not insured
■ For those prepared to take a calculated risk	■ Vulnerable to market risks
■ For those who don't want to pick their own stocks or bonds	■ Changes in value with the stock market or interest rates
■ Over the very long term, stocks tend to outpace other investments	■ A fee is charged for setting up an IRA
■ A professional is managing your money	■ There may be sale fees too
■ Dividends or earnings can be automatically reinvested in additional shares	■ Easy to neglect monitoring your fund's performance
	■ Better returns may be available elsewhere

Brokerage Houses

At some point down the road, if you feel confident enough about picking stocks and you've been making maximum contributions to your IRA account for several years, you might consider opening a "self-directed" IRA through a brokerage firm. You will manage the funds, but the broker will serve as custodian, collecting the commission on your buy and sell trades.

When your IRA is small, this type of account hardly pays since you don't have enough money with which to diversify. In other words, the amount is not sufficient to spread out over several different stocks or bonds. And, on top of that, the brokerage fees are high in relation to the size of your account. (See page 17 for a sample of commission fees.) If eventually, however, you decide to run your own

IRA, try doing it through a discount broker where the fees are substantially lower.

Zero Coupon Bonds *Good*

Because interest income is tax deferred in IRA and Keogh plans, Treasury zero coupon bonds are well suited to these accounts. For example, a person planning to retire in 1998 might invest $179.37 and have at retirement $1,000. If a person is able to invest $1,790, he or she will receive $10,000 in 1998.

Your IRA and the Tax Law

The 1986 Tax Reform Act reduced the number of people who can deduct the amount they put into an IRA every year. In the past, the entire $2,000 deduction was available to everyone. Now, only you may make a deductible IRA contribution of up to $2,000, provided neither you nor your spouse is an active participant in an employer-sponsored retirement plan and you are younger than age 70½ at the end of the year. Even if you or your spouse is an active participant in a plan, you may still be able to deduct IRA contributions. However, the maximum deduction is decreased when adjusted gross income (AGI) is over $40,000 for a married couple or $25,000 for a single person, and the deduction will be eliminated when AGI reaches $50,000 for a married couple or $35,000 for an unmarried person.

Hint: If you are divorced and receive alimony, you can make an IRA contribution even if all your income is from alimony, as it is treated as earned income.

Even if you are not eligible for the $2,000 deduction, do not abandon your IRA. It is still an excellent way to accumulate tax-deferred earnings for the day when you retire. At that time, you'll pay taxes on the amount you withdraw, but most likely you will then be in a lower tax bracket.

ADVANTAGES OF AN IRA

- Every dollar you contribute can be written off your tax return if you are not a part of a qualified pension fund or if your income is below $25,000 (single) or $40,000 (married).

- Penalties discourage IRA withdrawals prior to retirement.

- Interest or dividends are tax free until withdrawn.

DISADVANTAGES OF AN IRA

- If you cash in your IRA early, you will face stiff penalties.

- IRAs are not liquid. Although you can withdraw money, the penalties for doing so are stiff.

- IRAs may not be used as collateral.

Banks, brokers, and mutual funds all have charts showing how much you will be ahead with an IRA. We have reproduced one below so you can study the benefits. Keep in mind that the inflation rate is not factored in on these charts, so the benefits are not quite as wonderful as they appear on paper.

The IRA Connection

Investment performance in an IRA account far outstrips most similar investments made in the taxable world. This table shows the benefits of putting $2,000 per year in an IRA that compounds at 8 percent, compared to putting the same amount in a taxable investment, assuming a 28 percent tax bracket.

WHAT is your TAX bRACKET?

IRA VS. TAXABLE INVESTMENT

Years	IRA	Taxable Account
5	$11,924	$11,867
10	28,130	27,568
15	50,627	48,343
20	82,369	75,831

You may have use of your IRA dollars once a year for a sixty-day period through a procedure called a **rollover** in which you actually take money out of one IRA account and put it into another one. But beware: Unless your assets are in another IRA within sixty days, you will have to pay both income tax and the added 10 percent penalty tax. Some people find a rollover useful if they need cash for less than sixty days.

Two of the most helpful booklets on IRAs are available for free. Contact your nearest office of the Internal Revenue Service for a copy of Publication 590, *Individual Retirement Arrangements (IRAs)*.

For a copy of *Plan Tomorrow Today*, write to: Investment Company Institute, 1600 M Street NW, Washington, DC 20036.

A Keogh Plan

If you are self-employed, either part-time or full-time, you should try to take advantage of the tax benefits offered by a Keogh plan. Anyone who earns income from his or her own business, profession, or skill is entitled to participate in a Keogh as well as in an IRA.

Note: Even if you have an IRA or a private pension plan set up in which to save salaried income, you may still have a Keogh plan in order to shelter that portion of your income that comes from being self-employed. If you are completely self-employed, however, you can still have both an IRA and a Keogh.

As with an IRA, you have a number of custodian choices: banks, savings and loans, brokerage houses, mutual funds, and insurance companies. And, as with the IRA, all your contributions are deductible from your federal income tax, and the interest in your account accumulates free of taxes. The same early withdrawal penalties apply as well.

Here's where the two plans differ: In a Keogh you may contribute up to 20 percent of what you earn through self-employment—before tax deductions—for a total of $30,000 annually. If you have high self-employed income, that's a much better deal than the $2,000 IRA maximum. On the other hand, if you're self-employed part-time, the 20 percent ceiling may be rather low.

13
Your 401(k) Plan

I've got all the money I'll ever need if I die by four o'clock.
—Henny Youngman

One relatively painless way to make certain you have money to get you past four o'clock and through retirement is the 401(k) plan. Offered by many employers to employees, this savings plan has become increasingly popular since it was authorized by Congress in the early 1980s. Not only does it provide employees with an automatic way to save for retirement, it also reduces and defers taxes.

With this type of retirement savings plan, also known as a **salary-reduction plan,** you contribute a certain amount of your annual salary to a special retirement account that has been set up by your employer with an authorized institution. This contribution is deducted from your paycheck, so you don't even miss the money. The amount deducted is listed separately on your W-2 form, but is not included in the amount listed for "wages, tips, other compensation." In other words, your contributions are made with pre-tax dollars. Your contribution reduces your reportable salary, which in turn reduces your federal income tax liability.

Most plans let employees decide where to invest their contributions. The typical choices are the company's stock, a stock mutual fund, a long-term bond fund, a money market fund, or a guaranteed fixed-rate income fund. Generally, you can move your money among the different investments at least once a year.

Although taxes are postponed until you start receiving the money, there is a 10 percent penalty tax for withdrawing money before age 59½.

Hint: Even if you are eligible for a tax deduction on your IRA, contribute to a 401(k) too if it's offered where you work. The maximum you can put into an IRA is only $2,000 a year, whereas the ceiling on a 401(k) is much higher and indexed for inflation: The 1990 ceiling was $7,979.

Each company that offers employees these plans has its own special designs. Ask your employee benefits officer to explain yours. Many companies match all or part of their employees' contributions.

Withdrawing and Borrowing

You can withdraw funds before age 59½ only if you're facing a financial hardship—for example, if you need to pay funeral or medical expenses for a member of the family or, in some cases, to pay for a principal residence or avoid eviction. The regulations are very stringent. To be eligible for a hardship withdrawal, you must prove that you can't meet your needs by borrowing from a bank or tapping other savings. However, many plans do permit borrowing. Rules on borrowing vary widely from plan to plan. Ask what the interest rate on loans is and how long you have to pay it back.

Hint: The interest rate is often lower than what a bank will charge and, of course, your interest payments accumulate to your account and not to a bank.

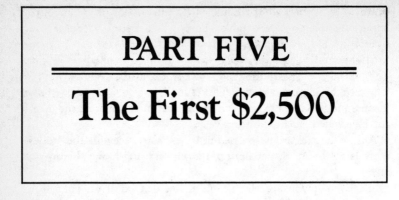

PART FIVE
The First $2,500

14
Bank Money Market Deposit Accounts

Top-notch protection *and* liquidity. This almost unbeatable combination is available when you open a **money market deposit account (MMDA)** at your bank. Authorized on December 14, 1982, these accounts are insured for up to $100,000 and also pay money market rates without locking up your money for any given period. They are, in fact, an insured variation of the regular money market mutual fund discussed in Chapter 7.

Rules and Regulations

Originally, federal law required a minimum balance of $2,500 to open and maintain an MMDA. In 1985 the minimum was dropped to $1,000, and today there is no required minimum at all. Many banks, however, set their own, with most at $2,000 or $2,500. Be sure to get this figure before opening an account.

Keep in mind that both yields and penalties imposed for falling below the minimum vary widely from bank to bank. Once again, it pays to shop around—some banks let you transfer funds to an ordinary checking account by telephone or ATM (automatic teller machine).

With a bank money market deposit account, you can write only three checks per month (to a third party) against your balance, although you are allowed to withdraw money in person as often as you like—as long as you keep your minimum balance. Usually there is no minimum amount on the size of the checks.

The interest rate on these accounts is generally, but not always, half a percentage point below that of Treasury bills. Banks adjust the rate periodically along with changes in short-term interest rates. Of course, they tend to remain competitive with the money market mutual fund rates. Both, after all, are aggressively going after your savings dollars.

There is a key difference in the way in which interest is paid to depositors of money market deposit accounts and to shareholders in a money market mutual fund. Money market mutual funds *must* pay out most of their earnings to the fund's shareholders (and a percentage is retained to cover the cost of operating the fund). Although banks are not required to pay out all that they earn, they are obliged by law to post the interest rate they will pay each month. Although banks can pay whatever rate they want, in general you can expect bank rates to be slightly lower, since the money is insured.

If you're an active investor or a saver who tends to move money around a lot, this multipurpose account could be extremely useful. You get immediate access to your money and it allows you to use other bank services as well.

Because terms and rates do vary so from bank to bank, as well as from region to region, nationwide shopping for MMDAs has become an important investment trend. And, not surprisingly, several publications have sprung into existence to help you find the best rates, which could turn out to be anywhere from Kansas City to Des Moines to Lake Charles.

MUTUAL FUND OR BANK FOR YOUR MONEY MARKET?

Money Market Mutual Fund

- Best for those who switch from bonds to stocks to money market funds
- Best for those who dip into their funds often
- You can write as many checks as you like ($150 or $500 minimum per check is common).
- No service charges
- Not insured

Bank Money Market Deposit Account

- Best for savers
- Best for those who do not dip into their money very often
- You can write only three checks per month to third parties.
- You can withdraw money in person as often as you like.
- Insured up to $100,000
- Service charges
- Penalties for dropping below minimum balance

BANK MONEY MARKET DEPOSIT ACCOUNTS

For Whom

- Investors who know they can maintain the minimum balance
- Those who want high market rates and instant liquidity
- Those seeking a safe parking place for their savings or emergency money

Minimum

- Determined by individual banks; the average is usually $2,000 to $2,500

Safety Factor

- Very high
- Insured up to $100,000

Advantages

- High interest rates

- You can transfer money to checking account (three preauthorized transfers per month).

- You can withdraw in person as often as you like.

- You can get money out easily if interest rates drop.

Disadvantages

- Some banks have penalties for withdrawal.

- You must maintain a minimum balance, determined by the bank.

- You can write only three checks per month.

- If balance falls below minimum, interest rate may revert back to passbook rate.

- If balance falls below minimum, some banks will pay no interest at all.

- If balance falls below minimum, some banks impose a monthly charge and may or may not pay interest.

Special Hints

- Find a bank money market deposit account that can be linked electronically to other accounts and to the bank's automatic teller machine network. Then you can write more than the three minimum checks since there is no limit on how often you can personally make transfers. In other words, if the accounts are connected, you can keep most of your money in the high-paying MMDA and transfer funds into your checking account only as you need to.

- Select a bank that allows you to connect your MMDA to a brokerage account so you can buy stocks, bonds, and Treasuries via telephone.

- Look at the effective annual yield. That is easier to compare than deciphering each different bank's compounding methods.

- Find out if your interest rate will be lowered to passbook rate if your account falls below the required minimum. Find a bank that cuts the rate only for the days when your balance is below the minimum, not one that penalizes you for the entire week or month.

15
Stock & Bond
Mutual Funds

Buying shares in a mutual fund is often a good alternative to trying to pick from among the thousands of individual stocks available. For the small investor, the new investor, and the very busy investor, mutual funds offer diversity, professional management, liquidity, and relatively low cost. Compared with other similar investments, they also offer the possibility of price appreciation. Some funds have no minimum investment amount; for others it is as low as $500. You should have at least $2,000 before you participate in a fund for stocks, however, because in this type of investment there is a greater degree of risk than in money market mutual funds, CDs, and other vehicles we have already described. After all, the stock market, and your fund, could go down, not up, in price. That is the risk you take when purchasing a stock fund.

When you buy into a mutual fund you are actually purchasing shares of an investment trust or corporation. Your dollars are pooled with those of hundreds of other investors, and these combined monies are then invested and managed by professionals in large, diversified portfolios of stocks, bonds, and various money market papers. This diversification helps insulate you against wide fluctuations in the prices of individual stocks. A professional does the buying and selling.

Mutual funds are open-ended—that is, like stocks, shares are continually available and they can be bought or sold at any time. The actual price of a fund is determined at the end of the day and is based upon the total value of securities in the fund's portfolio.

Choosing a Stock Mutual Fund

Before beginning your search for the right fund, you should know the difference between load and no-load funds. **Load funds**, sold by stockbrokers and mutual fund salespeople, are "loaded" with a sales charge or fee. Commissions for the purchase or sale of the fund generally range from about 4 percent to 8½ percent of the total price. Keep in mind that this means the value of the fund must escalate by that amount before you can break even. Although there is no difference in the performance of a load fund over a no-load fund, you might as well find one without a commission and save the difference for investing. But sometimes people like to buy load funds because they come recommended by their stockbrokers; they find it easier to let the brokers do the fund selection for them.

No-load funds have no sales commissions; you purchase shares directly from the fund itself, not through a stockbroker. For a complete list of no-load funds, consult:

✝ *Guide to Mutual Funds* ($5.00)
Investment Company Institute
1600 M Street NW
Washington, DC 20036

This annual guide lists nearly 3,000 load and no-load mutual funds under 22 different investment objective categories.

The Individual Investor's Guide to No-Load Mutual Funds ($22.95)
American Association of Individual Investors
625 North Michigan Avenue
Chicago, IL 60611

Includes low-load funds that have a load or fee of 2 percent or less. Provides name of portfolio manager, total return figures, and level of risk involved.

The Handbook for No-Load Fund Investors ($49)
by Sheldon Jacobs
The No-Load Fund Investor, Inc.
Box 283
Hastings-on-Hudson, NY 10706

The "bible" of the industry, this annual guide provides advice on selecting the right fund, when to sell, how to switch funds, etc. The *Handbook* with a monthly newsletter that keeps fund investors up-to-date is $109.

So, even if you go the route of a mutual fund, you're still not entirely free of decision making. Now you must, of course, decide which fund you want—there are over 2,000 to choose from! You can narrow your choice, however, by following these steps.

Step 1

Clarify Your Goals. Do you want a fund for income or for growth? Do you want a fund that consists primarily of stocks, bonds, or some of each? Do you want a high-risk speculative fund, or a more conservative one? Each fund has different investment objectives, so it is important that you understand these differences before making your selection. The fund's objectives are noted at the beginning of the **prospectus,** which is the official description of the fund required by the Securities and Exchange Commission. For example, a prospectus might read: "Our primary objective is safety of principal and long-term growth through the purchase of high-quality stocks in growth areas of the economy."

Step 2

Study the Types of Funds. Funds fall into several broad categories. Because of the boom in mutual funds over the past few years, you can select today from a broad range. There are funds that emphasize growth, others that focus on income. Some have tax-free holdings, others aim at capital appreciation or have speculative holdings. In selecting a fund, be realistic about how much time you can afford to spend watching it go up and down. The more speculative its portfolio, the more you need to keep your eye on it in order to know when to get out when its value starts to fall.

Here are the basic types of stock funds.

- **Growth Funds.** These seek long-term capital appreciation by buying stocks in companies that will grow faster than the rate of inflation. Dividend payments are usually low. Within this category there are the following:
  1. **Aggressive or speculative funds.** These also seek maximum profit, but at a fast rate, which is often achieved by taking greater risks, by selling short, or even by borrowing money for additional leverage. These are also known as maximum capital gains funds.

2. **Industry funds.** These specialize in one type of stock, such as energy stocks.

- **Income Funds.** These invest primarily in corporate bonds and are not concerned with growth. Some invest in high-dividend stocks. For more on bond income funds, see pages 52–56.

- **Growth and Income Funds.** Also called "balanced funds," these maintain portfolios that combine stocks and bonds and emphasize low risk. These portfolios often consist of leading companies that pay high dividends.

- **Municipal Bond Funds.** These are designed for tax-exempt income. (See pages 35–36.)

- **Money Market Funds.** (See pages 29–35.)

- **Specialized Funds.** We will not discuss these funds, for they tend to be very speculative in nature and are not generally appropriate for the under $5,000 investor. If you are interested in any of them, your broker can help you find the best. They include option funds, hedge funds, venture capital funds, gold funds, and so forth.

Step 3

Study Management's Performance Record. Rating services publish the performance records of mutual funds over various time periods. These appear in several financial publications including *Barron's* and *Money* magazine. Consult these and other publications at your library or broker's office.

Once you have decided what type of fund you want, follow these easy tips in making your final selection.

- Find a fund that has at least $100 million in assets. If a fund is too small it may not be able to pay for first-rate analysts and a research staff. An exception to this rule is a small fund that is part of an umbrella organization, which is also known as a family of funds.

- Check the fund's annual performance rating in the sources listed on page 33.

- Find out from the fund's prospectus how long the fund has been in existence. Don't select one that has not had enough time to post a track record.

- Look for a fund that is increasing in size, not decreasing.
- Select a fund that is part of a family of funds and has switching privileges (more on switching below).

All in the Family

Even after you have selected a fund, you may be nervous about how it will react to sudden changes in the economy, interest rates, or the market. One way to resolve this dilemma is to keep your money in a family of funds that offers more than one type of fund under the same corporate roof. You should look for a fund family that has a bond fund, a stock fund, and a money market fund so that you can switch your money from one fund to another as the economic climate changes. Pick a fund in which switching is free of charge or offered at a very nominal amount. The prospectus will tell you if you are limited to a certain number of switches per year. Make certain, too, that you can do your switching over the telephone.

How do you know when to switch? It requires time and study, but in general:

- When interest rates fall, keep your money in a mutual fund that has a stock portfolio.
- When interest rates rise, switch to a money market fund.
- When you see the price of the equities held in your fund going down, switch to a money market fund.

Through a family of funds you can take advantage of surges in prices and fluctuations in interest rates. There are about sixty fund families on the market today, and they offer more than four hundred individual funds. The largest are Fidelity and Vanguard.
Hint: No one fund should be regarded as economically viable for all times. The market is cyclical, constantly changing, so never make an investment and think that's it. You must continually monitor all investments, including mutual funds.

If you feel ready to try switching among a family of funds, you may want to examine one of the newsletters that advises readers on how and when to move among the various mutual funds. This list is not a recommendation, only a guide to what is available.

90

Telephone Switch Newsletter ($137/year; monthly)
2100 Main Street
Huntington Beach, CA 92647
800-950-8765

Mutual Fund Investing ($99/year; monthly)
7811 Montrose Road
Potomac, MD 20854
800-722-9000

16
Ginnie Mae Funds

These funds aim for high income and minimum risk and more often than not succeed. Ginnie Maes, short for Government National Mortgage Association (GNMA), are actually pools of mortgages backed by the Federal Housing Administration (FHA) or the Veterans Administration (VA). They are the only securities—except for those issued by the U.S. Treasury—whose principal and interest are backed by the "full faith and credit of the U.S. government." (*Caution:* The guarantee by the government protects you from only one thing: default by homeowners. In other words, it guarantees that interest and principal will be paid—but it guarantees neither the value of fund shares nor the interest rate. Your shares will indeed fluctuate in price, for like bond funds, when interest rates rise the value of Ginnie Mae mutual funds falls, and vice versa. That's why you should buy Ginnie Mae mutual funds only if you can hold your shares long term, thus smoothing out the fluctuations in interest rates.) You can buy a Ginnie Mae certificate for $25,000 through a broker, or buy shares in a Ginnie Mae mutual fund for as little as $1,000.

A Ginnie Mae begins when a home buyer receives, from a lending institution, a mortgage insured by the FHA or VA. The lender then combines this mortgage with many others into a pool worth at least $1 million. This certificate—a mortgage-backed security—is then sold to a broker, who in turn sells pieces of it, known as certificates, to individual investors and mutual funds. The minimum amount is $25,-000. As the homeowners make monthly payments on their loans, owners of certificates receive a share of the principal and interest payments on a monthly basis. Although these are suitable for investors seeking a steady stream of income, *they are not totally risk free.* When interest rates fall, homeowners rush to pay off their mortgages ahead of schedule and refinance at lower rates. When that happens, investors receive their principal and interest payments sooner than planned. They then face the problem of reinvesting this money at the then prevailing rates, which of course are lower than when they purchased their certificates.

A Ginnie Mae fund operates quite differently from the certificates. You purchase shares of the fund. The fund manager buys and sells Ginnie Mae certificates in much the same way a bond fund trades bonds. Therefore, *your yield is not fixed* in a fund. It will rise and fall in relation to interest rates. Your fund's success also depends on the ability of the manager to buy and sell certificates at the best time.

Caution: Some funds allow a percentage of their portfolio to be invested in riskier real-estate-backed securities such as Freddie Macs, Fannie Maes, or nonguaranteed mortgages in order to keep their yields high. Others remain cautious and invest only in Ginnie Mae certificates and Treasury bonds. A fund's prospectus will spell out these details for you.

Before selecting a fund, read the prospectus to learn what's in the fund's portfolio. The prospectus will also tell you if the fund has check-writing privileges, if it charges for dividend reinvestment, or what its sales fees and other charges are.

GINNIE MAES

For Whom

- Investors who want a high yield

Where to Purchase

- Directly from fund or stockbrokers

Fee

- Load funds charge a sales fee that ranges from 3 percent to 8.5 percent.

- No-load funds do not charge a sales fee, but there may be other hidden costs.

Safety

- Relatively high

Minimum

- $1,000 for funds, $25,000 for certificates

Advantages

- Yields tend to be slightly higher than U.S. Treasury issues.

- Provide income on monthly basis

- Can reinvest income in additional fund shares

Disadvantages

- Yields are not guaranteed and could fall.

- Some funds are allowed to sell options against their portfolios to keep the yields high; this adds to the risk level.

- Price of fund's shares can drop.

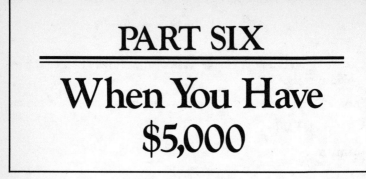

17
Stocks: Growth & Income

Almost everyone at some point in his or her life entertains the idea of buying a stock, a piece of American industry. Many actually do more than just think about it—over 20 percent of the U.S. population owns stocks.

According to a recent study done by the Securities Industry Association, individual investors buy and sell an average of 157.6 million shares a day.

There are four compelling reasons why, at the $5,000 level, you, too, should consider buying stocks:

- Over the long term, stocks tend to outperform bonds.
- Stocks offer the possibility of price appreciation.
- Stocks offer the possibility of keeping ahead of inflation.
- Stocks, especially those paying high dividends, are excellent sources of income.

Hint: If you have never owned a stock, read "What Is a Stock" in Chapter 11.

Are You Ready for the Market?

Prior to selecting stocks for your own portfolio, you must have money set aside for an emergency. At least three months' worth of living expenses should be safely stashed away in a liquid investment, such as a money market mutual fund, a money market deposit account, or a certificate of deposit. Once this has been accomplished and you have accumulated $5,000, you're ready to go. (Although it *is* possible to invest in the market with smaller amounts of money, in order to establish a truly diversified portfolio you need a base of about $5,000.)

First, *determine your investment goals*. Are you seeking a stock that pays a high cash dividend, or would you prefer to buy one that will appreciate substantially in price? Do you want liquidity—that is, the ability to get money back when you want it, or are you content to wait for long-term growth? Your goals make a difference, because no one stock offers high dividends, instant liquidity, spectacular appreciation, plus stability.

The Risk Factor

But, before you invest, keep in mind that while many stocks are profitable investments and return handsome rewards in terms of capital appreciation, they also can decline in price. *There is no guarantee that you will make a profit.* Careful selection is essential.

The ABCs of Stock Selection

When you have accumulated $5,000 *and* established an emergency nest egg, you can prudently consider investing for either growth or income through purchase of common stocks. A **common stock** is a fractional share of ownership in a corporation. For example, if a corporation has one million outstanding shares and you buy one share, you then own one-millionth of that corporation.

This ownership enables you to participate in the fortunes and growth of the corporation. If the corporation prospers, its earnings (which are expressed as earnings per share) will rise, which in turn tends to make the price of the stock rise. Simply put, the corporation's value has increased. Generally, some part of these earnings is shared with stockholders in the form of a cash dividend that is paid out four times a year.

If you believe that certain corporations or industries will flourish in the coming years, try selecting several common stocks in these areas as an investment for income, growth, or a combination of the two. As a general rule, don't put more than 10 percent of your funds into the stock of any one company and no more than 20 percent in any one industry.

Remember that stocks can also decline in price and you should try to confine your selections primarily to blue chip companies, that is, large, well-financed, and established corporations with secure positions within their industry.

Here are five key standards to use in judging a stock.

1. Earnings per share should show an upward trend over the last five years. If, however, earnings declined for one year out of five, this is acceptable, provided the overall trend continues to rise.

Earnings per share, simply defined, is the company's net income (after taxes and money for preferred stock dividends) divided by the average number of common stock shares outstanding. You will find it listed in the company's annual report or in professional materials such as *Value Line* or Standard & Poor's *Stock Guide,* available at your library or in any broker's office.

2. Increasing earnings should be accompanied by similarly increasing dividends. You should study the cash dividend payments over the last five-year period. In some cases a corporation will use most of its earnings to invest in future growth, and then dividends may be quite modest and rightly so. But even in these cases, some token dividend should be paid annually. Ideally, a company should earn at least $5 for every $4 it pays out.

In conjunction with the company's dividend, you should note its **yield,** which is the current dividend divided by the price of a share.

It is listed in the newspaper along with the dividend and other statistics. The yield should be higher in a stock you purchase for income than in one selected for potential price appreciation (see sample stock listing, later in this chapter).

3. Standard & Poor's rates each company's financial strength. For you, the $5,000 investor, the minimum acceptable rating should be A—.

4. The number of outstanding shares should be at least ten million. Marketability and liquidity depend upon a large supply of common stock shares. Ten million shares ensures activity by the major institutions, such as mutual funds, pension funds, and insurance companies. Institutional participation helps guarantee an active market in which you and others can readily buy and sell the company's stock.

5. Study the company's price to earnings ratio (P/E ratio). This ratio is found by dividing the last year's earnings per share (or the current year's estimated earnings) into the current price of the stock. The **P/E ratio** is one of the most important analytical tools in the business. It reflects investor opinion about the stock and about the market as a whole. For example, a P/E of 11 means investors are willing to pay 11 times earnings for that stock. A P/E of 11 indicates greater investor interest and confidence than a P/E of 7 or 5, for example.

A P/E ratio under 10 is considered conservative and, depending upon the company, its industry, and your broker's advice, you can feel comfortable with a P/E of 10 or less. As a company's P/E moves above 10, you begin to pay a premium for some aspect of the company's future. For example, a P/E ratio above 10 may very well be justified by outstanding prospects for future growth, by new technological advances, or by worldwide shortages of a product that the company produces.

Basically, the P/E ratio is the measure of the common stock's value to investors. A low P/E of 5 or 6 usually means that the prospects are clouded by uncertainty.

Similarly, a P/E of 14 or 15 indicates a keen appetite on the part of investors to participate in that company's future.

Whatever stock or stocks you decide to buy, you want to get in at the lowest possible P/E—before there is a lot of investor interest and the P/E is bid up. No one can say exactly what ratio you should accept, and it is here that your selection process and your broker's advice become important.

WHAT STOCKS SHOULD YOU INVEST IN?

- Sound industries that provide basics, such as food or utilities. These tend to hold their own even during recessionary periods.

- Companies that are industry leaders, especially if you are a beginning investor

- More than one company and more than one industry. If you invest in one company and it turns out to be a mistake, you will have lost everything.

- Shares traded on a major exchange: NYSE or ASE. This gives you some added protection because in order for a stock to be listed the company must file financial statements with the SEC and the stock exchange and meet certain standards. They are also easier to buy and sell.

How to Read a Financial Page

Once you own stocks, you will want to know how they are doing—whether they are going up or down in price. To find out, you can read the market quotations in the daily newspaper.

You will find your stock listed under the name of its exchange—the New York Stock Exchange, American Stock Exchange, Over-the-Counter, and so forth. Here's how it works, using IBM—International Business Machines Corporation—as an example (prices are quoted in fractions of a dollar, so 107⅝ means $107.675 per share):

52 Week				Yield	P/E	Sales				
High	Low	Stock	Div	%	ratio	100s	High	Low	Last	Chg
123⅛	93⅛	IBM	4.84	4.5	15	26586	109	104⅝	107⅝	+2¼

- The first two columns tell the highest and the lowest prices per share for the last 52 weeks. In the case of IBM, they are 123⅛ and 93⅛.
- The next column gives an abbreviated form of the stock's name. Here it is IBM.
- Then comes the annual dividend, if any. For IBM it is $4.84.
- Following the dividend is the stock's yield, which is given as a percentage. To determine the yield, divide the dividend by the closing price: $4.84 divided by $107.675 = 4.5%.
- After the yield comes the P/E ratio or price divided by earnings. You will note that earnings are not listed in the paper. The P/E here is 15.
- The number 26586 in the next column indicates the number of shares traded that particular day. It is listed in hundreds, so 2,658,600 shares of IBM were traded on that day.
- The next two numbers, 109 and 104⅝ tell how high and how low the stock traded that day. In other words, during the course of the day, some stock traded as high as 109 and some trades were made for as little as 104⅝ per share. The following column shows the price of the final trade that day, and the final column illustrates the change in the closing price from the prior day. In this case it was 107⅝, which was 2¼ (or $2.25) over the preceding day's closing price. Sometimes there will be a minus sign, indicating it fell in price. If there's no plus or minus sign, then the closing price was the same as the day before. *Note:* These figures do not include the broker's commission.

Buying Stocks

Once you have decided to become involved with the stock market, the next issue to resolve is whether to use a broker or to select your own stocks. Generally speaking, if you have never owned a stock before, it is probably more prudent to get help from an experienced professional than to go it alone.

Selecting a Broker

Knowing when and how to seek the advice of an expert is a critical part of being a successful investor. If you've never had a broker (or, if you've had one you did not like) you can find the right one by doing some investigative work well in advance. Plan on spending three to four weeks to locate the broker who is right for you.

Start by thinking about how you selected your doctor or lawyer. Someone else probably suggested them to you. Getting the recommendations of friends and colleagues whose judgement you respect is one of the best ways to find a good broker. Ask your boss, your banker, your uncle, or your pediatrician if they have a broker they like.

After gathering several names, call and make appointments with each one. Tell them the amount of money you have to invest. Not all brokers are interested in small accounts, yet many are. Those who are realize that a small account obviously has the potential of becoming a larger one over time. A number of the major "full service" houses, such as Merrill Lynch, Paine Webber, and Shearson Lehman Hutton, are indeed willing to open small accounts. Merrill Lynch has a special program for small investors, described on page 20. You will also find that reliable regional brokers are set up to handle accounts of all sizes, and they are eager to help local investors. If you feel you don't need investment advice, you can save on commissions by buying through a "discount" broker, such as Charles Schwab. In either event, a broker must execute the final buy or sell transaction for you.

Before you interview your broker candidates, prepare a list of questions to ask them. It should include these four items, plus anything else that concerns you:

1. *Do you handle accounts of this size?* You certainly don't want to use a broker who is uninterested in $5,000.

2. *Can you give me one or two references?* Avoid any broker who says no.

3. *How long have you been a broker?* Any broker tends to look good in a good market. You want an experienced person who knows how to handle money in bad times as well as good.

4. *How should I invest my $5,000?* Beware of the broker who advises you to put it all in one stock, or even all in the market. Unless you have specifically said the total amount is to be invested in stocks, the broker should advise you to diversify.

For additional details on how to select a broker you may want to check with your library for a copy of *How to Talk to a Broker* by Jay J. Pack. New York: HarperCollins, 1985.

Going It Alone

Once you have gained some feeling for the market, you may want to plunge right in and do your own stock selection. If you decide to follow this course, you must be prepared to regard it as a learning experience, for *it is very unlikely you will pick all winners*—even the pros don't manage to do that. So, at first, avoid putting more money than you can afford to lose in the market.

The best way to minimize your risks, of course, is to be well informed. To be your own broker you must be prepared to spend a significant amount of time reading about the economy and about individual companies, as well as the major industries.

Where You Can Find Information

1. *Specialized financial periodicals and newspapers* are excellent sources of information on the general economic climate and the stock market. In particular: *Barron's, The Wall Street Journal, The New York Times, Financial News Daily,* and *The Chicago Tribune* among the newspapers. Good magazines are: *Forbes, Business Week, Financial World, Fortune, U.S. News,* and *Money.* We have mentioned previously *Better Investing,* the monthly magazine of the National Association of Investment Clubs. Devoted to investment education, it analyzes stocks and covers various views on investments.

2. *Brokerage firms have a wealth of research material.* The large houses will send you some material, even if you are not a customer—at least for a limited period. Many have copies of newsletters on display in their retail offices. Although much of this information is generally known, you can still gather ideas, and certainly it is valuable for background data.

3. *Annual reports of corporations are an important source.* Write or call any company you are considering investing in for a copy and then read the section in this book called "How to Read an Annual Report" in the appendix.

4. *Standard & Poor's New York Stock Exchange Reports,* a large looseleaf volume, is regarded as a bible in the financial world. It contains one page, both sides, on each company listed on the NYSE. S&P also publishes similar volumes for the American Stock Exchange and for over-the-counter stocks. The material is revised periodically. For each corporation you will find a summary description, the current outlook, and new developments, plus a ten-year statistical table.

5. *Standard & Poor's Stock Guide* is a small monthly booklet containing basic data in condensed form on 5,000 stocks: price range, P/E ratio, dividend history, sales, an abbreviated balance sheet, earnings, and the S&P rating. A similar monthly booklet is put out covering bonds. For further details on all S&P publications, contact:

> Standard and Poor's Corporation
> 25 Broadway
> New York, NY 10004
> 212-208-8000

6. *Value Line Investment Survey* contains the most comprehensive coverage of stocks. *Value Line* follows 1,700 companies and their industries. Each industry is updated quarterly. Stocks are ranked on the basis of timeliness for purchase and safety. A subscription to this service also includes a separate weekly analysis of the market and general economic situation plus an in-depth discussion of one stock recommended for purchase. Contact:

> Value Line, Inc.
> 711 Third Avenue
> New York, NY 10017
> 212-687-3965

7. *Financial newsletters can be helpful, but they vary enormously in reliability and success as far as their advice goes.* Before subscribing to any newsletter, try to locate copies at your library or by contacting the publisher. Many will send a free copy or offer trial subscriptions at a reduced rate.

There is also a service that rates the advisors. *Hulbert Financial Digest* is a monthly newsletter that tracks and ranks fifty of the stock market newsletters based on their performance in recommending stocks. One issue costs $5; a five-month subscription is $37.50; a full year's subscription is $135. Contact: Hulbert Financial Digest, 316 Commerce Street, Alexandria, VA 22314; 800-443-0100.

8. *Sale and purchase of a company's stock by officials of the corporation is one way to determine trends in the price of the stock.* Newsletters chart this so-called insider trading. If copies are unavailable at your public library or broker's office, write to the publisher and ask for a free sample and information about trial subscriptions.

- *The Insiders.* Norman Fosback, editor. 3471 North Federal Highway, Fort Lauderdale, FL 33306; 1-800-327-6720; semimonthly; $49/year.
- *Value Line Investment Survey* (see p. 102).

Your Investment Achilles Heel

Even with rational research and thoughtful planning on your part, you may still fall prey to one or more of the ubiquitous emotional traps that lie in wait in the investment field.

Every investor has areas of vulnerability. If you recognize yours, it's then possible to eliminate many errors and reduce misjudgments. Here are the five most common pitfalls small investors make when buying and selling stocks.

1. Tendency to hold on to securities too long, hoping a poor performer will turn around

2. Reacting immediately to bad news and selling too soon

3. Refusing to sell and take the profit because you feel you can squeeze out a few more points

4. Refusing to take a profit because of capital gains tax, even when the stock is fully valued

5. Avoiding selling a stock you inherited because of sentimental feelings

One way to avoid these and other pitfalls is to have a game plan, to know what your financial objectives are and then stick to them.

SEVEN STOCK MARKET DO'S

1. Know whether you're investing for long-term appreciation or immediate income, and select stocks that match your goal.

2. If you're investing long term, remember that the market fluctuates daily and the item to focus on is earnings, not price.

3. Know about the industry. Don't purchase a medical technology stock or a high-tech issue without first studying the industry.

4. Read the company's annual and quarterly reports before buying.

5. Stick with companies that are leaders within their industry.

6. Look for companies with a proven record of consistent growth.

7. Be patient.

18
Annuities

An annuity is a form of savings account offered by an insurance company that guarantees regular payments to the purchaser, either for a stated period of time or for life. In order to receive this money, you, the annuitant, make payments called **premiums** to the insurance company, either all at once in a **single premium,** or over time through an **installment premium.**

The basic purpose of an annuity is to provide income while you are alive, whereas life insurance is intended to provide income to your heirs.

There are two basic kinds of annuities: fixed and variable. In a **fixed annuity,** the amount you invest (your **principal**) earns interest at a fixed rate that is guaranteed for a specified time period. It could be for one year, or for as long as four or five years or more. When that time is up, your money is reinvested at a new rate, which could be more or less than the initial rate. Most fixed annuities have a floor below which the return will not drop. And your principal is guaranteed at all times.

When you take your money out of a fixed annuity (usually on a monthly or quarterly basis) you receive a guaranteed dollar amount based on your age, sex, and the type of payments you've elected. **Hint:** The key disadvantage of this type of annuity is that it may not keep pace with inflation.

On the other hand, **variable annuities** take inflation into consideration. You, not the insurance company, decide whether to invest your premium payments in stocks, bonds, or money market accounts. That means your return is variable, fluctuating daily depending on the performance of the investments you select. And, of course, monthly payments vary as well, based on the value of your account, the amount you put in, and how long you're expected to live. Although this type of annuity offers potentially greater returns than its fixed-rate cousin, your return is not guaranteed. This type of annuity is suggested for those who like to follow the market.

There are two other terms you should be familiar with. You can purchase an annuity long before retirement, known as a deferred annuity, or you can wait until you retire and purchase an immediate annuity. Here are the key differences:

- With an **immediate annuity,** your income checks from the insurance company will start arriving soon after purchase. An immediate annuity is ideal when you receive a lump-sum payment from a company pension plan.
- With a **deferred annuity,** payouts don't begin until sometime after purchase—typically several years after you've paid all the

premiums. This annuity is suggested only for those who know they can leave their money in the plan and for those who are at least several years away from retirement.

Taking Money Out

At retirement, or when you want to begin receiving payments, you must make a payout decision. Among the choices are:

- **Straight life,** or lifetime only, which pays until the annuity holder dies. This is recommended for those who want to enjoy every penny they've saved. If you die in the first year of payments, the contract ends. On the other hand, if you live to be 100, the annuity will still make regular monthly payments. This type of plan offers the highest monthly payments.
- **Life and period certain** pays the owner and/or a beneficiary for a specified minimum number of years, usually 10, 15, or 20. For example, in a ten-year certain annuity, if you die after four years, a beneficiary will receive monthly income for another six years. This plan pays a smaller monthly dollar amount than straight life.
- **Joint and survivor** pays as long as the annuity holder *and* the beneficiary are alive. This offers even smaller monthly payments.

Selecting a Fixed-Rate Annuity

- Contact an insurance broker. Ask about plans that have a bailout provision giving you 45 days after the guarantee period ends in which to cash out or transfer money to another annuity without a penalty if the rate of return falls by a certain amount—typically 1 percent.
- Beware of any plans that entice investors with exceptionally high initial rates.
- Make certain that when money is rolled over after the guarantee period, the new rate is the same as the rate being paid to new customers.

- The safety factor of fixed-rate annuities depends on the financial health of the insurance company. Select a company rated A or A+ by A.M. Best, or AAA by Standard & Poor's, two independent rating services. And steer clear of any company that keeps more than 10 percent of its portfolio in high-yield or so-called "junk" bonds.
- Fixed-rate annuities are tracked by Comparative Annuity Reports, Box 1268, Fair Oaks, CA 95628. A list of the 100 top-ranked annuity programs is available for $10.

Selecting a Variable Annuity

- Again, check the A.M. Best and S&P ratings.
- Deal only with a company that provides a choice of at least five or six different funds, as well as the option to switch among funds at any time, either at no charge or for a minimal flat fee.
- Look for the best performing annuity mutual funds. Total returns are tracked by Lipper Analytical Services, which does not take into account sales charges. Lipper's results are given in the financial pages of major newspapers. Or ask a salesperson for the most recent monthly survey by Variable Annuity Research & Data Service (VARDS) of Miami. VARDS tracks the total returns of more than 500 annuity funds, subtracting management fees in calculating performances.
- Ask about the surrender charge—if money is withdrawn during the early years of the plan. A typical surrender charge starts at 7 percent for money withdrawn during the first year and diminishes to zero after seven years. Many companies allow penalty-free withdrawals of 10 percent of an account's asset value; however, this money will be taxed.

For Whom

- Those receiving a lump sum from a pension plan
- Anyone wishing to supplement retirement income

Where to Purchase

- Insurance brokers, stockbrokers, and financial planners
- Commercial banks, credit unions, savings and loans

Fees

- Vary widely with plan. Typical example:
  1. Front-end sales charge of 1 percent to 10 percent
  2. Annual fees of $5 to $35 per year to maximum of 1½ percent of account value
  3. Early withdrawal penalties: 7 percent declining to zero in 7 years

Safety

- Relatively high with solid insurance company
- Select only a company rated A or A+ by A.M. Best & Co.

Minimum

- $5,000; additional payments may be as little as $100

Advantages

- Earn tax-deferred income
- Forced way to save
- Guarantees regular income in the future

Disadvantages

- Various tax penalties apply
- Better yields may be available elsewhere
- Fixed-income plans may not keep pace with inflation
- In a variable plan, investments may not make money

Appendix

"Dear Shareholder"

How to Read an Annual Report

Just looking at the pictures and skimming the headlines in an annual report won't really help you evaluate the investment potential of a company, but armed with a little knowledge ahead of time, you can glean a lot of useful material from even the thinnest report.

The typical annual report consists of a letter to the stockholders from the president or chairman, a description of the company's business operations, detailed financial tables, a mass of footnotes, and a statement by an outside auditor.

It's quite easy to get lost in this forest of financial statistics, yet by developing your own search system—one that can be used with any annual report—you will soon have a basic comprehension of the business you may wish to invest in.

A word of caution: Don't let slick, glossy paper, artistic photographs, and two-tier pullouts impress you unduly. These can be merely the work of a good public relations firm and not a true measure of the company. A simple presentation of the facts and an open divulging of financial statistics are what counts.

Step One

With an annual report, it's best to start at the back and review the material presented by the auditor-certified public accountant. This generally consists of a brief statement to the effect that the financial material was prepared in accordance with "generally accepted accounting principles" (GAAP). If that's it, then the company has been given a clean bill of health. If, however, the auditor's statement contains

111

hedge clauses such as "the results are subject to," then beware. That's accountant-ese for an unresolved problem, perhaps a legal action that carries serious financial implications for the company. Frequently it implies that a ruling against the firm may lead to lower earnings than those printed in the annual report. Some statements are even less subtle: "Uncertainties exist as to the corporation's ability to achieve future profitable operations." All auditor's reservations should be noted before reading the rest of the annual report.

Step Two

At the beginning of nearly every annual report is the president's or chairman's letter to the stockholders. Traditionally this is management's chance to comment on last year's results and the outlook for the future. It also reflects the tone and direction of the company as viewed by management. Yet you should be aware of hidden caveats here, too: "All development went along as expected except for . . ." or, "We will meet our stated goals on target unless. . . ." Think of these as warning signals. Approach the statement from management as an opportunity to learn how they think and plan.

Step Three

Footnotes comes next. They often define terms and conditions actually used in the financial pages, such as a change in accounting methods. The footnotes will also alert you to the fact that earnings are up because of a windfall that won't occur again next year, or that legal action is pending.

Step Four

After you've waded through the footnotes, turn to the income statement, usually located in the middle of the report. It will give you a good idea of what direction sales and earnings took during the year as compared with the previous year. If both earnings and sales went up during the year, it certainly is good news. It's even better if earnings rose faster than sales. The income statement also gives you a picture of the company's cash flow position. Cash flow consists of net profits plus depreciation. To arrive at a measurement of cash flow, divide the cash flow figure found in the statement by the amount of long-term debt. Anything under 20 percent is generally regarded as unsuitable—although there are exceptions.

Step Five

You should now turn to the profitability of the company. The margin of profit is determined by taking the operating income (i.e., income before payment of income tax) and dividing it by total sales. Certain industries, such as supermarket chains, have low profit margins—1 percent to 2 percent—whereas most industrial companies have margins in the neighborhood of 5 percent. Look for companies with stable and rising profit margins.

Step Six

The balance sheet, traditionally a two-page spread, contains the company's assets (everything the company owns) on the left and its liabilities (everything the company owes) on the right. Things that can quickly be converted into cash are called current assets, while the debts due within one year (which can be paid out of current assets) are called current liabilities. It is important to realize that the balance sheet offers the company's financial picture only at a single point in time. Like a snapshot, it gives you an instant idea of the corporation's strength. Its purpose is to show what the company owes and owns. Among the things to check are:

- How much cash is included under current assets. If the amount is shrinking, you must question what is draining this money from operations.

- The next working capital figure, a key number in determining a company's financial health. You can calculate this by subtracting current liabilities from current assets. This is what actually would be left over if all current debts were paid off; therefore it shows the resources available within the company to cover short-term debts. You can determine if this dollar amount is at a safe level by converting it into a ratio. Simply divide current assets by current liabilities to get the current asset-to-debt ratio. Most stock analysts like to see a 2:1 ratio. The net working capital is a crucial figure for investors to monitor, for if it drops there may not be sufficient money for expansion or future growth.

- The quick ratio, another means of determining financial strength, can be derived from the balance sheet. To arrive at this number, subtract inventories from current assets and divide by current liabilities. This figure should be more than one; in other words, current assets less inventories should at least be equal to if not greater than current liabilities. The quick ratio is a way to find out if a company is able to take care of its current debts as they mature.

- The company's ability to meet its obligations is another measure of financial strength. This, too, can be determined from the balance sheet by finding the debt-to-equity ratio. Divide long-term debt by total capitalization; both figures are generally given. (Total capitalization consists of long-term debt, common stock, capital surplus, retained earnings, and preferred stock.) A manufacturing company is in good shape if debt is 20 percent or less of capitalization. Higher debt ratios—40 percent to 50 percent—are acceptable in some industries, such as utilities. A high debt-to-equity ratio indicates that the company is probably borrowing to keep going—an acceptable position if sales are growing too and if there is an adequate amount of cash to meet payments. Beware, however, if sales start to fall, too.

There are many more sophisticated ratios you can obtain from working with the annual report, but these six steps are a good beginning. Don't forget to look for the elementary facts, too. They're just as important and include:

- The size of the company. What are its assets? A large company is less likely to face a sudden failure.

- The age of the company. Older firms have weathered good times and bad.

- The management. Are they experienced and are they personally investing in the company?

- The company's earnings. Are net earnings per share going up? Check the previous five years' record and look for trends in net sales, too.

There are other important indicators in the annual report. So for more extensive instruction on how to make sense out of the report, contact any Merrill Lynch Pierce Fenner & Smith office and ask for a copy of "How to Read a Financial Report."

The important thing to keep in mind is that you must compare these key indicators from one year to the next. Is the company's net working capital up or down? What is the trend in the changes in the debt-to-equity ratio? One year's statistics are not sufficient evidence on which to judge a company.

Nine Easy/Painless Ways to Save

Granted, it's a great deal more fun to spend money on a romantic dinner in a restaurant or for a winter vacation in the Caribbean, yet to make certain you can always dine out and travel in style, you need to save. Extra dollars not only make dreams come true, they also let you sleep at night. If you want college for your kids, a house of your own, and a retirement nest egg, build your savings by following these nine easy tips. You'll find saving is infectious.

1. *Make savings your first bill.* Once a month when you pay your bills, write a check to deposit in your money market fund or savings account at your bank or credit union. Start by saving 1 percent of your take-home pay the first month; then increase the amount by ½ percent each month. By the end of the year you'll be socking away 6½ percent per month.

2. *Use automatic savings plans.* If you don't see it you won't spend it. Arrange for a certain amount—it can be as little as $50—to be taken out of your paycheck and automatically transferred to your savings or money market fund at a bank or credit union. Ask if your employer also has a payroll savings plan for E.E. Savings Bonds. *Alternatives:* Have your bank automatically transfer a certain amount from checking to savings each month; or have funds automatically withdrawn from your checking account and put in a money market fund.

3. *Leave credit cards at home.* Pay with cash or by check. You'll spend less and you'll avoid monthly interest charges on unpaid credit card balances.

4. *Defer taxes.* Money in an IRA, Keogh, 401(k), or other qualified retirement plan grows tax-free until withdrawn. You can fund these plans by making small contributions several times a year rather than trying to pay in one large lump sum. *Alternatives:* Investments that are fully or partially tax exempt: municipal bonds, municipal bond mutual funds, EE Savings Bonds, and U.S. Treasury securities.

5. *Contribute to a stock purchase plan.* Many companies allow employees to contribute part of their salary to buy the firm's stock through automatic payroll deductions.

6. *Reinvest stock dividends.* See pages 18–19 for details.

7. *Keep making payments.* When you've paid off a mortgage or a loan, continue to write a check for the same amount (or at least half the amount) every month and put it into savings. You've learned to live without that money, so now you can sock it away.

8. *Save your change at the end of the day.* Small amounts add up quickly. Put your nickels, dimes, and quarters in a jar before going to bed.

9. *Treat yourself.* Saving is smart but not always immediately gratifying. The payoff is sometimes several years away. Now and then spend a little on yourself. It will make saving much easier.

Index

The letter "t" following a number indicates that the information is contained in a table.